THE
GREEN THUMB
HARVEST

THE

GREEN

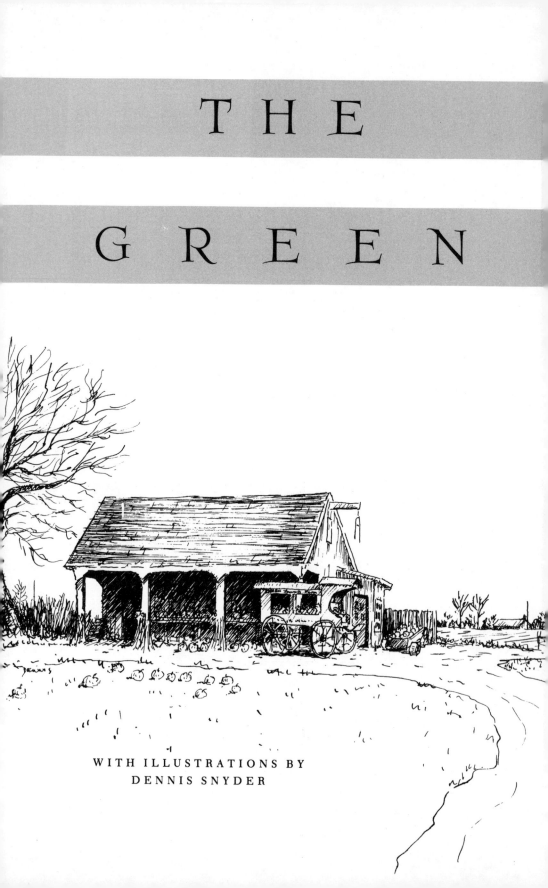

WITH ILLUSTRATIONS BY
DENNIS SNYDER

THUMB

HARVEST

JOHANNA AND PATRICIA HALSEY

VINTAGE BOOKS
A DIVISION OF RANDOM HOUSE
NEW YORK

A VINTAGE ORIGINAL, FIRST EDITION MAY 1984

Introduction Copyright © 1984 by Craig Claiborne
Copyright © 1984 by Johanna and Patricia Halsey
All rights reserved under International
and Pan-American Copyright Conventions.
Published in the United States by Random House, Inc.,
New York, and simultaneously in Canada by Random House
of Canada Limited, Toronto.
Library of Congress Cataloging in Publication Data
Halsey, Johanna. The Green Thumb harvest.
"A Vintage original."
1. Cookery (Fruit)   2. Cookery (Vegetables)
3. Cookery (Herbs)   I. Halsey, Paticia.   II. Title.
TX811.H35   1984   641.6'4   83-40376
ISBN 0-394-72372-4
Book design by Iris Weinstein
Manufactured in the United States of America

To Mom and Dad
Whose Light Always Shines Forth

OUR THANKS TO:

all those people who generously shared their recipes,
all our friends for their discriminating palates,
Dennis Snyder for the illustrations,
Jack Hangen and the Agawam staff for their patience,
Gloria Safir and Jason Epstein for their encouragement,
Anne Freedgood for her continuous guidance,
a terrific Green Thumb crew,
all the earth angels who supported us through thick and thin,
the two best brothers two sisters could ever have.

FOREWORD

It is true that the small territory on the eastern end of Long Island referred to as "the Hamptons" is often called the most fashionable resort in America. I have for the past twenty years taken small comfort in this thought, for, to me, it is simply the place I call home.

When I first moved out there two decades ago, it was not because it was a chic place to be, nor did I think of it in terms of food. My reasons for going there were about as obvious and mundane as all get out. It was simply a desire to get away from the noise and confusion, the hustle and bustle of Manhattan, to walk on weekends those miles of sandy beach and to revel in the summer sun. It did not take me long to learn, however, that I had landed right in the midst of a food lover's paradise. And most of the foods I discovered were not wholly surprising. I was not startled to find a first-rate poultry farm about a mile or so away, to realize that I could find freshly caught striped bass and fluke and freshly harvested scallops to be purchased less than a ten-minute drive from my kitchen door.

But within a decade of my arrival I discovered a phenomenal source for green things. It was a small barnlike structure just off the highway, surrounded by farmland and owned by a handsome, smiling man named Raymond Halsey, whose family had settled in the town of Water Mill over three hundred years ago. The place was called simply The Green Thumb, and it was staffed by the Halsey family. The wonder of this enterprise was not merely the first strawberries of the summer, the first sweet white and/or yellow corn of the season, and the usual prosaic vegetables of the territory—cauliflower, green

peppers, potatoes, and the like. Within a short while this
Tiffany among garden places carried a wondrous bewilder-
ment of fresh herbs, the likes of which would be hard to find
in a single setting in any given metropolis in America. When
summer came, I found the place amply endowed with the
most precious herbs—not just parsley, sage, rosemary and
thyme, but things like fresh coriander, savory, hot green and
red chilies, fennel, fresh basil, both green and red, arugula,
upland cress, and mustard cress.

I have always felt that some uncertain destiny was deter-
mined to plant my feet on ground where people love to cook
and to think and talk about food, and I have found it in the
Hamptons ("This my heart's country," if I may quote a local
poet, the late John Hall Wheelock, who lived not far away). I
am not an uncommonly social sort, but the tables at which I
have dined and the kitchens that I have visited have been
generally notable for their inspiration. And this book, I feel, is
representative of the taste and enthusiasm of my "neighbors."

After all, it is The Green Thumb cookbook. And the Halseys
have numbered among their clientele all the greatest (and
most famous) cooks of the region.

CRAIG CLAIBORNE

CONTENTS

THE
GREEN THUMB
HARVEST

INTRODUCTION

The roadside vegetable stand in Water Mill, New York, known as The Green Thumb opened in 1961, but the land on which it stands and the fields behind that supply it have been in the Halsey family since 1640, shortly after Water Mill was settled by colonists from New England. We are the eleventh generation of Halseys to harvest this soil.

Water Mill is one of the string of little villages that stretch in a line along the South Fork of the eastern end of Long Island from Southampton to Montauk—the area that has come to be known to the rest of the world as "the Hamptons," although the year-round inhabitants are more apt to think in terms of individual towns. Long before it was resort country, it was farm country, and in recent years most of the farming has been potatoes.

Our father, Ray Halsey, was originally a potato farmer, but by the time he was in his mid-twenties, he and our mother, Peachie, had four children, and he was forced to face the fact that, with the price of potatoes, single-crop farming was not going to support their needs. One morning in early summer, as he was plowing the land on the edge of the Montauk Highway, which is still the only direct route along the South Fork, he started counting the cars coming out from New York City. That was some years before the real rush to the Hamptons began, but still there were a good number, and it occurred to him that if he could tempt one car in every five to stop, he might find a way to make farming pay. He and Peachie discussed the idea of giving over some of the land to a variety of vegetables to be sold on the spot, and Granny Halsey, the matriarch of the clan, gave the project a name—The Green Thumb.

That first summer Ray planted thirty-five acres with lettuce, peas, corn, beans, tomatoes, peppers and eggplants. A local boy helped pick in the early morning and then opened the stand in a leisurely way around nine. On weekends, when as it turned out at least one car in every five did stop, our parents tended the stand and we children sold rides on our ponies.

That summer was a success, and so was the next. Ray began to experiment with many different kinds of vegetables and herbs and to turn more and more land over to them. In 1968 he sent to Holland for a huge greenhouse, and as soon as it was assembled, The Green Thumb moved into high gear. The greenhouse made it possible to start seeding in February and to continue through the spring and summer, moving the seedlings out to the fields as soon as they were large enough and keeping successive plantings of some of the same crops, like lettuce, going from early May until September, so that the vegetables we sold were always young and fresh. We also began to pick three or four times a day and bring the fresh vegetables in to the stand. In 1969 we built a larger Green Thumb, and the original stand became a walk-in cooler out back.

The Green Thumb now harvests more than one hundred acres of vegetables, including fifteen kinds of green and red lettuce, ten kinds of sweet corn, ten kinds of squash, a full variety of herbs, chocolate and golden as well as red and green peppers, sugar snaps and snow peas, lemon cucumbers, purple string beans, cranberry beans, black radishes, and the original small white egg-shaped eggplants, to name some of the more unusual. There are ten people working at the stand and twenty in the fields, but it is still very much a family business. Peachie, who has become synonymous in most people's minds with The Green Thumb because of her warm relationship with the customers, manages the stand. Ray and our brothers, Bill and Larry, oversee the crops, battle the insects and the elements, and try out new ideas, like organic and hydroponic farming. Patti doubles in the stand and in the fields, and Johanna has taken on the flowers—snapdragons, zinnias, statice, marigolds —that we now also grow and sell.

Our customers come back year after year, from the city as "the season" starts and from the neighboring towns as the days warm up. And each year there are new ones, who become as interested in what we are doing and how we grow our vegetables as our old friends are. Many of them take one of Ray's weekly "farm tours" on a tractor, which moves slowly through the fields while Ray, standing in the back, describes the characteristics and requirements of the different crops as the tractor drives past them, and hands around samples.

In return, our customers tell us about the recipes they have invented using our vegetables and fruits. About two years ago we got the idea of collecting them in a cookbook. We asked our customers to give us their favorites, we added some of our own, and we spent the winter and the next spring and summer cooking and tasting. This is the result. It is not a vegetarian cookbook. Although vegetables, herbs or fruit are an important ingredient in every recipe, many include meat, fish or poultry as well. And because The Green Thumb has only three seasons—we open in late May and close just before Christmas —our book is divided into three seasons as well. The creators of the recipes appear at the bottom of each recipe; recipes with no name are our own.

JOHANNA HALSEY
PATRICIA HALSEY
WATER MILL,
NOVEMBER 1983

FARM TOUR

ASPARAGUS
2 pounds serve 4 people.
Basic cooking time: 10–12 minutes.
Serve with melted butter and lemon juice or with Hollandaise
sauce.

FRESH LIMA BEANS
3 pounds unshelled serve 4 people.
Basic cooking time: 15–25 minutes.
Serve with butter.

STRING BEANS
1 pound serves 4 people.
Basic cooking time: 8–15 minutes.
Serve with butter, butter and lemon juice, or an herb butter,
for example, tarragon or fennel.

BEETS
1 pound serves 4 people.
Basic cooking time: 45 minutes.
Serve with butter and lemon juice, or in a béchamel sauce with
a little grated nutmeg.

BROCCOLI
1 pound serves 4.
Basic cooking time: 8–15 minutes.
Serve with butter and lemon or with Hollandaise sauce.

BRUSSELS SPROUTS
1 pound serves 4.
Basic cooking time: 10–20 minutes.
Serve with butter and pepper or lemon juice.

CABBAGE
1 pound serves 4 people.
Basic cooking time: shredded, 5–8 minutes;
                    wedged, 12–15 minutes.

CARROTS
1 pound serves 4 people.
Basic cooking time: 10–15 minutes for sliced or young carrots.
Serve with butter and chopped parsley or some other herb, or
    serve mashed with cream, butter and parsley.

CAULIFLOWER
1 medium head serves 4 people.
Basic cooking time: whole head, 15–20 minutes;
                    flowerets, 8–10 minutes.
Serve with butter, with butter and lemon or with béchamel or
    cheese sauce.

CELERIAC (Celery Root)
1 pound serves 4 people.
Basic cooking time: whole 30–60 minutes;
                    cubed, 10–15 minutes.
If cooked whole, peel and mash with butter. Perhaps combine
    with one third mashed potato, or add some Dijon mustard
    and lemon juice, salt and white pepper.
If cooked cubed, serve with butter.

COLLARDS
1½ pounds serve 4 people.
Basic cooking time: 8–10 minutes.

CORN
1 ear of corn serves 1 person.
Basic cooking time: 3–5 minutes in boiling water.
Serve with butter, salt and, if you like, black pepper.

EGGPLANT
2 pounds serve 4 people.
Basic cooking time: cubes sautéed in olive oil, 5–10 minutes; baked whole, 35–50 minutes at 350°.
If baked, serve with sour cream or fresh cream, seasoned well with salt and pepper.

FENNEL
1 pound serves 4 people.
Basic cooking time: 10–15 minutes.
Serve with butter or with a mild cheddar cheese sauce.

KALE
2 pounds serve 4 people.
Basic cooking time: 8–15 minutes.
Serve with butter and herbs or with a cheese sauce.

KOHLRABI
1 pound serves 4 people.
Basic cooking time: 15–20 minutes.
Serve with butter or in a béchamel sauce.

LEEKS
1 pound serves 4 people.
Basic cooking time: 10–20 minutes.
Serve with butter or in a béchamel or Mornay sauce.

MUSHROOMS
2 pounds serve 4 people.
Basic cooking time: sautéed, 5–7 minutes.
Add garlic and a touch of vinegar, if you like.

OKRA
1 pound serves 4 people.
Basic cooking time: simmered, 10–15 minutes.
Serve with fresh lemon juice or in a tomato sauce.

ONIONS
1 pound serves 4 people.
Basic cooking time: small, white, 15–20 minutes;
large, 40 minutes.
Serve in a béchamel sauce.

PARSNIPS
1 pound serves 3–4 people.
Basic cooking time: 15–20 minutes.
Serve with butter or in a béchamel sauce.

PEAS
3 pounds serve 4 people.
Basic cooking time: 10–15 minutes.
Serve with butter or with butter and chopped herbs,
  for example, mint.

SNOW OR SUGAR PEAS
1 pound serves 4 people.
Basic cooking time: steamed, 5–8 minutes;
sautéed 5 minutes.
Serve in cooking juices or with butter.

PEPPERS
1 pound serves 4 people.
Basic cooking time: sautéed, 5–10 minutes.
Serve with a little lemon juice or wine vinegar.

POTATOES
2 pounds serve 4 people.
Basic cooking time: boiled, 15–20 minutes;
baked, 1–1½ hours.
Serve with butter and parsley or with sour cream and chives.

PUMPKINS
1–1½ pounds serve 4 people.
Basic cooking time: simmered, 25–30 minutes
  (3 × 2-inch chunks)
Serve with butter.

RUTABAGA
1 pound serves 4 people.
Basic cooking time: 15–30 minutes.
Toss in butter or mash with cream and butter.
  Also serve in a béchamel sauce.

SALSIFY
1 pound serves 4 people.
Basic cooking time: simmered for 15–20 minutes,
  then sautéed in butter for 5 minutes.
Serve with butter or Hollandaise sauce.

SPINACH
2 pounds serve 4 people.
Basic cooking time: 6–8 minutes.
Serve with butter and lemon or in a cream or cheese sauce. Try
  a little grated nutmeg. Or sauté cooked and drained spinach
  with a little chopped garlic in olive oil; add lemon juice.

SQUASH
1 summer squash serves 1 person;
1 pound winter squash serves 2–3 people.
Basic cooking time: summer squash—
                simmered, 10–15 minutes; sautéed,
                10 minutes.
                winter squash—
                simmered, 20–30 minutes; baked, 40–60
                minutes at 350°.
Serve summer squash with butter.
Serve winter squash with butter, or mash it with cream and
  fresh herbs or with butter and cinnamon.

SWEET POTATOES, YAMS
1–2 pounds serve 4 people.
Basic cooking time: simmered, 30–40 minutes;
                baked, 45–60 minutes at 350°.
Serve peeled and mashed with butter and a dash of cinnamon.

SWISS CHARD
2 pounds serve 4 people.
Basic cooking time: simmered, 20–25 minutes;
                    steamed, 30 minutes.
Serve with butter and fresh herbs or in a rich cream
  or cheese sauce.

TOMATOES
1½ to 2 pounds serve 4 people.
Basic cooking time: broiled, 10–15 minutes.
Serve with fresh basil or onions.

SPRING

Asparagus Canapés

About 80 canapés

1 pound fresh asparagus spears, trimmed
1 large loaf bread, thinly sliced
8 ounces Roquefort cheese
8 ounces cream cheese
1 tablespoon mayonnaise
1 beaten egg
½ cup melted butter

Cook the asparagus until tender. Drain and cool. Set aside. Cut the crusts off the slices of bread and roll each out flat. Combine the cheeses, mayonnaise and egg. Blend thoroughly. Spread some of the mixture on each slice and top with an asparagus stalk. Roll up and cut into thirds. Brush each piece with the melted butter. Place on an ungreased cookie sheet and freeze.

Bake frozen in a preheated 350° oven for 15 minutes.

(SANDRA FOX)

Creamy Asparagus Soup
4–6 servings

2 tablespoons butter
1 medium onion, finely chopped
3 tablespoons all-purpose flour
2½ pints chicken stock
Salt and freshly ground black pepper to taste
½ teaspoon celery salt
¼ teaspoon nutmeg
1 pound asparagus spears, trimmed and chopped
1¼ cups light cream
¾ cup grated Gruyère cheese
2 tablespoons chopped fresh parsley for garnish

Melt the butter in a saucepan, add the onion and sauté until soft and transparent.

Remove from the heat and sprinkle with the flour. Stir well, gradually adding the chicken stock. Add the salt, pepper, celery salt, nutmeg and asparagus. Return to the heat and bring to a boil, stirring constantly. Turn down the heat, cover and simmer for 20–30 minutes, or until the asparagus is tender.

Remove from the heat, purée and reheat gently. Stir in the cream and blend thoroughly. Ladle into individual bowls, sprinkle with cheese and garnish with parsley.

Gourmet Vegetable Salad
8–10 servings

12 asparagus spears, trimmed and cut into 1-inch lengths
1 medium broccoli, broken into flowerets
¾ pound green beans, trimmed and cut into 1-inch
  lengths
1 cucumber, peeled and thinly sliced
1 medium sweet red pepper, chopped
2 shallots, minced
1 14-ounce can marinated artichoke hearts, drained and
  quartered
2 tablespoons freshly squeezed lemon juice
2 tablespoons white vinegar
2 teaspoons anchovy paste
1 cup mayonnaise
½ cup half-and-half
Chopped fresh parsley for garnish

Steam the asparagus, broccoli and beans separately until each is almost done, 8–12 minutes. Run each under cold water to stop the cooking process and drain well.

Combine the steamed vegetables, cucumber, red pepper, shallots and artichoke hearts in a large bowl and set aside.

Combine the lemon juice, vinegar, anchovy paste, mayonnaise and half-and-half, and blend well. Pour the dressing over the vegetables and stir thoroughly. Cover and marinate in the refrigerator for 24 hours. When ready to serve, sprinkle with chopped parsley.

(CLAIRE ODELL)

Asparagus Supreme

6 servings

3 tablespoons butter
2 tablespoons all-purpose flour
1 cup milk
1 cup grated cheddar cheese
¼ teaspoon salt
Freshly ground black pepper to taste
1½ pounds fresh asparagus spears, trimmed
4 hard-cooked eggs, sliced
½ cup slivered toasted almonds
Buttered bread crumbs

Preheat the oven to 350°. Butter an 8 × 13-inch pan.

Melt the butter in a heavy saucepan over low heat. Stir in the flour. Slowly pour in the milk and cook until thick, stirring constantly. Add the cheese, salt and pepper and continue cooking until well blended.

In the prepared pan, alternate layers of asparagus, egg, sauce and almonds to make 2 layers. Sprinkle with the bread crumbs and bake, uncovered, for 30 minutes. Serve immediately.

(MRS. LAWRENCE GOURLAY)

Asparagi con Uova

6 servings

2 pounds fresh asparagus spears
3 bay leaves
Handful fresh dill
½ pound butter
6 eggs
¾ cup freshly grated Parmesan cheese
Freshly ground black pepper to taste

Line up the asparagus spears, and break off and discard the tough ends. Steam the asparagus in a small amount of water in a large covered pot with the bay leaves and dill for about 10 minutes.

While the asparagus is steaming, slowly melt ¼ pound of butter in each of 2 large frying pans over medium heat. Break 3 eggs into each frying pan and cook until done.

When the asparagus spears are cooked, divide them among 6 plates. Gently place a fried egg on top of the asparagus on each plate, along with some melted butter. Top with a generous amount of cheese and pepper. Serve immediately.

("A classic northern Italian dish . . . I first enjoyed this at my friend's castle in Trentino."—**NICHOLE DEJURENEV**)

Asparagus with Orange Sauce
4 servings

1 pound fresh asparagus spears
½ cup butter
Juice of 1 orange
1 teaspoon grated orange rind
1 tablespoon chopped fresh dill

Break off the tough ends of the asparagus spears and discard. Steam the asparagus for 10 minutes, or until tender.

Melt the butter in a saucepan over low heat. Stir in the orange juice, orange rind and dill. Cook the sauce until it is hot, and then pour it over the asparagus. Serve immediately.

PEAS, SNOW PEAS AND SUGAR SNAPS

E Z Dip

3 teaspoons butter
1 medium onion, finely chopped
8 ounces cooked fresh peas
10 walnuts, shelled and chopped
2 hard-cooked eggs, sliced

Melt the butter in a heavy skillet over low heat; add the onion and sauté until soft and transparent. Place all the ingredients in a food processor or blender and purée until smooth. A great dip for crackers or fresh vegetables.

(NANCY MINEROFF)

Mt. Kenya Safari Club Champagne Soup

6 servings

1 pound fresh peas, shelled
2 leeks, diced
2 carrots, scraped and diced
2 medium onions, diced
2 cups water
27½ ounces chicken consommé
1 pint heavy cream
Salt and freshly ground black pepper to taste
6 jiggers champagne or white wine

Place the first 6 ingredients in a heavy saucepan and cook until soft. Pour the mixture into a blender or food processor and purée. Return to the saucepan and heat thoroughly. Just before serving, add ½ pint of the heavy cream, and salt and pepper. Beat the remaining cream.

Ladle the soup into bowls and add 1 tablespoon of whipped cream and 1 jigger of champagne or white wine to each bowl. Serve piping hot. This soup is also delicious without the champagne!

("This recipe was developed by a chef at the Mt. Kenya Safari Club—where VIP names in diplomatic, royal and Hollywood circles are commonplace—not too far from the big-game viewing lodges."—**EUNICE JUCKETT**)

Chicken with Sugar Snap Peas

2 servings

½ *pound chicken breasts, skinned, boned and cubed*
5 *teaspoons cornstarch*
¼ *cup peanut oil*
½ *pound fresh sugar snap peas or snow peas,*
    destringed
1 *tablespoon dry sherry or dry vermouth*
1¼ *teaspoons sugar*
½ *cup chicken broth*

Toss the chicken in 2 teaspoons of the cornstarch and let stand.

Heat the oil in a wok or skillet. Add the chicken and cook for 1 minute, tossing while cooking. Add the snap peas and cook for 1 minute.

Combine the sherry and sugar and add to the pan. Stir the remaining cornstarch into the broth and add to the chicken mixture. Cook over low heat, stirring occasionally, until the sauce thickens. Serve over a bed of rice.

(LILIA COLLINS)

Cold Chicken Salad

8 servings

2 pounds chicken breasts, skinned and boned
Salt and freshly ground black pepper to taste
4 tablespoons butter
¼ pound fresh snow peas, destringed and blanched
1 14-ounce can hearts of palm
½ cup chopped scallions (both green and white parts)
2 tablespoons chopped fresh basil
2 tablespoons chopped fresh chives
2 tablespoons chopped fresh parsley
1 cup Mustard Vinaigrette Sauce (recipe follows)
Boston lettuce leaves
12 cherry tomatoes, halved

Season the chicken breasts with salt and pepper. Melt the butter in a skillet, add the chicken and sauté over medium heat about 3 minutes on each side, until just cooked. Let cool. Cut into 1-inch cubes and set aside in a large bowl.

Slice the snow peas and hearts of palm into thin strips. Add them to the chicken, along with the scallions and herbs. Pour the vinaigrette sauce over the salad and toss well. Cover and refrigerate for several hours before serving.

To serve, mound the chicken salad on a bed of lettuce leaves and surround with the tomatoes.

MUSTARD VINAIGRETTE SAUCE
1 cup

1 egg
⅓ cup olive oil
1½ teaspoons freshly squeezed lemon juice
1 teaspoon Worcestershire sauce
¼ teaspoon freshly ground black pepper
2½ teaspoons imported mustard, such as Dijon

Break the egg into a blender or food processor and process until smooth. Add the oil slowly. Blend in the remaining ingredients, turning the machine on and off twice.

(NANCY TARSHIS-GALDSTON)

Ginger Sugar Snaps
4–6 servings

1½ pounds fresh sugar snap peas
3 tablespoons butter
1 tablespoon minced fresh ginger
2 teaspoons soy sauce

Trim the ends of the sugar snap peas and pull off the strings. Rinse well. Set aside.

Melt the butter in a heavy skillet over medium-low heat. Add the ginger and sauté for 2 minutes. Add the peas and continue cooking for 3 minutes. Stir in the soy sauce and cook for another 2 minutes. Serve immediately.

Rhubarb-Apricot Soup

8 servings

½ cup sugar
4 cups water
1 3-inch cinnamon stick
¾ cup dried apricots
3 cups diced fresh rhubarb
3 tablespoons cold water
1 pint fresh raspberries, or 1 box frozen raspberries,
    thawed and drained
1 tablespoon freshly squeezed lemon juice
Grated orange rind and sliced fresh strawberries for
    garnish

Combine the sugar, water, cinnamon and apricots in a sauce-pan. Bring to a boil and simmer for 5 minutes. Add the rhubarb and simmer until the rhubarb is barely tender, about 5 minutes. Cool.

Add the cold water, raspberries and lemon juice. Adjust the sugar to taste. Cool.

Garnish with grated orange rind and/or sliced strawberries.

(JUDITH LISS)

Rhubarb-Strawberry Compote

4–6 servings

1 2-inch strip orange peel
2 pounds fresh rhubarb, cut into 1-inch pieces
1 cup sugar
½ cup water
5 whole cloves
1 pint fresh strawberries, washed, hulled and cut in half
   lengthwise
2 tablespoons Grand Marnier

Preheat the oven to 450°.

Place the orange peel on a small piece of foil and bake for about 10 minutes, or until the peel starts to curl. Remove from the oven.

Combine the orange peel, rhubarb, sugar, water and cloves in a heavy cast-iron pot. Cover tightly and simmer gently for approximately 4 minutes. Add the strawberries, cover the pot, turn off the heat and let cool.

When cool, add the Grand Marnier. Chill before serving.

(MRS. PAUL DUVIVIER)

Rhubarb and Banana Cream

6–8 servings

2 pounds fresh rhubarb, cut into 1-inch pieces
1 cup sugar
4 tablespoons water
2 ripe bananas, mashed
1 cup heavy cream
2 egg whites
2 tablespoons Grand Marnier

Place the rhubarb, sugar and water in a saucepan and cook, stirring occasionally, for 15 minutes, or until the rhubarb is soft. Remove from the heat and drain the rhubarb. Place in a mixing bowl and allow to cool.

When cool, stir the bananas and cream into the rhubarb.

Beat the egg whites and fold into the mixture. Slowly pour in the Grand Marnier and blend well. Chill for at least 4 hours before serving.

Sour Cream Rhubarb Coffee Cake

8–12 servings

½ cup sugar
½ cup chopped nuts
1 tablespoon sweet butter
1 teaspoon ground cinnamon
½ cup shortening
1½ cups brown sugar
1 egg, beaten
2 cups all-purpose flour
1 teaspoon baking soda
½ teaspoon salt
1 cup sour cream
1½ cups fresh rhubarb, cut into small pieces

Preheat the oven to 350°. Grease and flour a 9 × 13-inch baking pan.

Mix together the first 4 ingredients and set aside for topping.

Cream together the shortening, brown sugar and egg. Stir in the flour, baking soda and salt alternately with the sour cream. When thoroughly blended, add the rhubarb.

Pour the mixture into the prepared pan and sprinkle with the topping. Bake for 45–50 minutes, or until a knife inserted into the center comes out clean.

(MRS. LEROY KIBLER)

SPINACH

Spinach Dip

¾ pound fresh spinach, washed, dried and stems
  removed
1 cup sour cream
1 cup mayonnaise
1 tablespoon chopped fresh dill
½ cup chopped fresh parsley
½ cup finely chopped onions

Finely chop the spinach and place in a mixing bowl. Slowly add the remaining ingredients and mix thoroughly.

This dip looks attractive when served in a hollowed-out round loaf of pumpernickel bread. A great dip for bread chunks, raw vegetables and crackers!

(PAT SANDERS)

Spinach Salad

4 servings

2 medium onions, sliced and separated into rings
4 tablespoons olive oil
⅓ cup cider vinegar
2 tablespoons honey
Salt and freshly ground black pepper to taste
1 pound fresh spinach, washed, dried and stems removed
½ pound fresh mushrooms, sliced
3 hard-cooked eggs, crumbled

Sauté the onions in the oil until transparent. Remove from the pan and drain on paper towels.

Add the vinegar, honey, salt and pepper to the pan. Bring to a boil, stirring constantly. Remove from the heat and let stand for 1 minute.

Meanwhile, combine the spinach, mushrooms and eggs in a bowl. Pour the warm dressing over the spinach mixture and toss well. Add the onion rings and toss gently. Serve warm or at room temperature.

(SUSAN ACTON)

Spinach Soup
4–6 servings

2 tablespoons butter
1 onion, finely chopped
2 tablespoons all-purpose flour
2½ pints chicken stock
Salt and freshly ground black pepper to taste
½ teaspoon paprika
½ teaspoon nutmeg
1½ pounds spinach, washed, dried, stems removed and
*   coarsely chopped*
⅓ cup heavy cream

Melt the butter in a large saucepan, add the onion and sauté until soft.

Remove from the heat and sprinkle with the flour. Gradually add the chicken stock, salt, pepper, paprika, nutmeg and spinach, stirring constantly. Bring to a boil, cover and simmer for 20–25 minutes. Purée the soup in a blender or food processor.

Return to the saucepan and stir in the cream. Reheat gently, stirring frequently.

Armenian Symob Soup
10 servings

1 cup barley
2 pounds fresh spinach, washed, dried and stems removed
2 quarts chicken broth
4 tablespoons butter
3 cups chopped yellow onions
4 tablespoons fresh mint, minced
3 tablespoons cornstarch
3 tablespoons sugar
¼ cup water
1 pint unflavored yogurt
Fresh mint leaves for garnish

In a large pot, place the barley, spinach and chicken broth, and simmer, covered, for 2 hours.

Melt the butter in a skillet over low heat, add the onions and sauté until soft and transparent. Sprinkle in the mint, stir well and add to the spinach broth.

Combine the cornstarch, sugar and water in a small saucepan. Mix until smooth, and then stir in the yogurt. Heat, stirring constantly, until the yogurt begins to thicken and comes to a boil, then add to the spinach mixture. Blend well.

Pour into a large soup tureen and garnish with fresh mint leaves.

(BRENT NEWSOM, ANNEX RESTAURANT)

Spinach-Onion Pie

10 servings

2 tablespoons oil
1½ pounds fresh spinach, washed,
  dried and stems removed
Pinch of salt
3 large bunches scallions, chopped
  (including the green parts)
½ pound cottage cheese
½ pound feta, crumbled
6 eggs, lightly beaten
Salt and white pepper to taste
1½ cups flour (approximately)
1½ cups water
8 tablespoons butter

Preheat the oven to 350°. Pour oil into a 12 × 18 × 3-inch baking dish and swirl to coat.

Finely chop the spinach and place in a colander. Sprinkle with the salt. Add the scallions and squeeze the greens to rid of excess moisture.

Place the spinach mixture in a large bowl and stir in the cheeses and 3 of the eggs. Season to taste with salt and pepper and set aside.

Add enough flour to the water and remaining eggs to make a thin batter (it should be thinner than crêpe batter). Pour half of the batter into a baking dish and top with the spinach mixture. Dot with the butter. Pour the remaining batter on top. Bake for 1 hour, or until golden brown.

(BARBARA GOL)

Flounder Filet Rena

5 servings

10 small flounder filets
Salt and freshly ground black pepper to taste
1 pound fresh spinach, washed and stems removed
Dash of nutmeg
5 thin slices of cheddar cheese
4 tablespoons butter
½–¾ cup dry white wine

Preheat the oven to 350°.

Lightly season the fish with salt and pepper. Blanch the spinach in boiling water, drain and squeeze as dry as possible. Chop and season with nutmeg.

Arrange 5 slices of fish in a buttered baking pan. Cover each slice with a large spoonful of spinach, add a slice of cheese and cover with a second piece of fish. Dot with the butter and pour the wine over all. Bake for 20 minutes.

(ANN SOBOTKA)

Poulet Farci

4–6 servings

1 cup cooked fresh spinach, chopped
¾ cup ricotta cheese
¾ cup freshly grated Gruyère cheese
¾ cup freshly grated Romano cheese
8 ounces butter, softened
1 egg
1 egg yolk
Salt and freshly ground black pepper to taste
1 teaspoon chopped fresh oregano
½ teaspoon chopped fresh thyme
½ teaspoon chopped fresh marjoram
1 roasting chicken (about 3½ pounds),
   cut into serving pieces

Preheat the oven to 375°.

Combine the spinach, cheeses and butter in a bowl. Add the egg, egg yolk, salt and pepper. Mix thoroughly and set aside.

Combine the herbs and set aside.

Partially separate the skin from the chicken breast, legs and thighs. Stuff the spinach mixture under the skin.

Place the chicken pieces in an oiled baking dish and sprinkle with the herbs. Bake for 1 hour.

(ANN EDSON)

Spinach Loaf

4 servings

1 pound fresh spinach, washed and stems removed
1 cup heavy cream
1 egg
Salt and freshly ground black pepper to taste
½ teaspoon nutmeg
½ cup freshly grated Parmesan cheese
4 tablespoons butter

Preheat the oven to 450°.

Parboil the spinach, drain well and chop. Beat together the cream, egg, salt, pepper and nutmeg. Stir in the spinach.

Pour into a buttered gratin dish. Sprinkle with the Parmesan cheese and dot with the butter. Bake for 25 minutes.

("A favorite recipe of my grandmother's . . ."—**EDWARD DRAGON**)

Country Spinach

4 servings

3 tablespoons olive oil
3 tablespoons butter
3 cloves garlic, finely chopped
2 pounds fresh spinach, well washed and stems removed
2 teaspoons freshly squeezed lemon juice
Salt and freshly ground black pepper to taste
Sprinkling of freshly grated nutmeg

Preheat the oven to 400°.

Put the olive oil and butter in a large ovenproof casserole and place on top of the stove over a medium-low heat. When the butter has melted, add the garlic and sauté until soft. Remove from the heat.

Add the spinach, cover and bake for 10 minutes, stirring occasionally.

Mix in the lemon juice, salt, pepper and nutmeg, cover and continue baking for another 10 minutes, stirring occasionally. Remove from the oven and serve immediately.

(HARRIET VICENTE)

STRAWBERRIES*

Chilled Strawberry Soup
4–6 servings

1 pint fresh strawberries, washed and hulled
2 cups water
1 tablespoon honey
2 tablespoons maple syrup
1 cinnamon stick
Juice of ½ orange
Dash of nutmeg
Dash of allspice
2 cups sour cream or yogurt
½ cup dry red wine
Mint leaves for garnish

Put the first 8 ingredients in a saucepan and bring to a boil. Lower the heat and simmer, uncovered, for 10–15 minutes, or

*Always wash the strawberries before you hull; otherwise they will get soggy.

until the strawberries are soft. Discard the cinnamon stick and purée the mixture in a food processor or blender.

Chill the purée until serving time. At serving time, stir in the sour cream and wine, beating with a wire whisk to combine the ingredients well. Pour into glass bowls and garnish with a floating mint leaf.

Orange-Strawberry Chicken

4–6 servings

1 small chicken (2½–3 pounds), skinned and cut
   into 8 pieces
½ cup fruit preserves (plum or strawberry is excellent)
½ cup white vinegar
½ cup soy sauce
¾ cup orange juice
½ cup sesame oil
3 cloves garlic, minced
3 teaspoons minced fresh ginger
2 teaspoons ground cinnamon
2 oranges, chopped, with some peel
1 cup fresh strawberries, washed, hulled and chopped

Preheat the oven to 375°.

Place the chicken in a baking pan and dot with the preserves. Combine the vinegar, soy sauce, orange juice and oil in a bowl and pour over the chicken. Sprinkle with the garlic, ginger and cinnamon. Smother with the oranges and strawberries.

Bake, uncovered, for about 1–1½ hours, basting about every 20 minutes and turning the pieces twice.

Serve with brown rice or noodles.

(NINA COOPER)

Strawberry Rhubarb

6 servings

2 pounds fresh rhubarb, cut into 2-inch pieces
½ cup sugar
1 quart fresh strawberries, washed, hulled and halved

Place the rhubarb in a large pot with about 1½ inches of water. Pour ¼ cup of the sugar over the rhubarb and cover. Allow to simmer until soft and somewhat saucelike (approximately ½ hour).

Stir in the strawberries and the remaining sugar. Simmer over very low heat, stirring occasionally, for about 10 minutes. Remove from the heat. Serve either warm or cold.

(BARRY E. FALLIS)

Strawberry Crème Brulée

6 servings

6 egg yolks
4½ tablespoons sugar
Pinch of salt
3 cups light cream, scalded
2 teaspoons vanilla extract
¾ cup strawberry jelly
1 pint fresh strawberries, washed and hulled

Preheat the oven to 350°.

Beat together the egg yolks and sugar in a large bowl until thick and lemon-colored. Add the salt. Slowly stir in the cream. Add the vanilla and blend well.

Pour into a glass pie pan or porcelain quiche pan. Place the pan in a larger pan of hot water and bake for about 1 hour, or until a knife inserted into the center comes out clean. Cool, then chill thoroughly.

Melt the jelly in the top part of a double boiler. Dip the strawberries into the jelly and arrange them on top of the chilled *crème* mixture. Brush the remaining jelly on top as a glaze. A beautiful and delicious dessert!

(JUDY LITTLE)

Godiva Chocolate Mousse Cake
8–10 servings

CAKE
¼ pound Godiva baking chocolate
¼ pound sweet butter, cut into cubes
4 egg yolks
½ cup sugar
3 egg whites

FROSTING
¼ pound unsweetened chocolate
¼ pound sweet butter, cut into cubes
4 egg yolks
½ cup sugar
3 egg whites
1 tablespoon powdered cocoa
1 teaspoon confectioners' sugar
1 pint large fresh ripe strawberries, washed and hulled

Preheat the oven to 325°. Butter the sides and bottom of an 8-inch springform pan.

Place the chocolate and butter for the cake batter in one saucepan and the chocolate and butter for the frosting in another. Set each saucepan in a large skillet of boiling water. Keep the water at the simmering stage, and stir the chocolate and butter until the chocolate is melted.

In one bowl of an electric mixer, combine the egg yolks and sugar for the cake, and in another, combine the egg yolks and sugar for the frosting. Beat each batch until the mixtures are light and lemon-colored. Add each chocolate sauce to the corresponding egg mixture, stirring to blend thoroughly.

Beat the egg whites for each recipe until stiff but not dry. Add half of each batch of egg whites to the corresponding chocolate mixture and beat. Fold in the remaining egg whites.

Pour the chocolate mixture for the cake into the prepared springform pan and bake for approximately 60 minutes, or until a toothpick inserted into the center comes out clean. When the cake is done, transfer it to a rack and allow to cool for 15–20 minutes.

Turn the cake out onto a cake circle or plate. Allow to stand until thoroughly cooled. Frost the sides and top with the frosting. Sift first the powdered cocoa over the top, then the confectioners' sugar. Surround the cake with the whole ripe strawberries.

(**THE TRELLIS CAFE**)

Strawberry Mousse

8 servings

4 cups fresh strawberries
1 envelope unflavored gelatin
½ cup sugar
½ cup water
2 egg whites
Pinch of cream of tartar
1 cup heavy cream
1 tablespoon Cointreau
Additional strawberries and mint for garnish

Wash, hull, and pat the strawberries dry. Purée the berries a cup at a time in a blender or food processor and pour into a bowl. Repeat until all are puréed.

Combine the gelatin and ¼ cup of the sugar in a small saucepan. Stir in the water. Place over very low heat until the gelatin and sugar are dissolved, then cool the mixture.

When cool, stir the gelatin mixture into the puréed berries. Place the bowl in a pan filled with ice and water to speed setting.

Beat the egg whites with the cream of tartar until they are foamy white. Beat in the remaining sugar, 1 tablespoon at a time, until soft peaks form. Beat the heavy cream with the Cointreau in a chilled bowl until soft peaks form.

Fold the egg whites and whipped cream into the strawberry mixture, stirring until no streaks of white remain. Pour into a clear glass bowl. Refrigerate for at least 4 hours, or until set. Garnish with additional strawberries and fresh mint.

(LILIA COLLINS)

Fresh Strawberry Shortcake

8 servings

4 quarts fresh ripe strawberries
2 cups unbleached flour
2 teaspoons baking powder
½ teaspoon salt
¼ teaspoon ground nutmeg
⅓ cup butter, softened
1 egg or 2 yolks
⅓ cup milk
1 cup heavy cream, whipped

Preheat the oven to 450°.

Wash, then hull the strawberries. In a bowl, lightly crush 3 quarts of the strawberries. Cover the bowl with plastic wrap.

Sift together the flour, baking powder, salt and nutmeg. Work in the butter with your fingertips or a fork. Lightly beat the egg or the 2 yolks into the milk with a fork and then add, little by little, to the flour mixture until a soft ball has formed.

Turn out onto a floured board. Pat a bit and then roll out the dough so it will fit into an ungreased 9-inch round pan. Bake for 12 minutes.

Have ready a large, somewhat concave (so strawberries and juice won't spill out) cake plate. Remove the cake from the pan and with a clean towel hold the cake so that you can slice it in half horizontally. Put the lower half on the plate, butter it, and cover with crushed strawberries. Top with the second half, butter and cover with the remaining crushed strawberries. Serve with the remaining whole strawberries and the cream.

(PEGGY BUCKWALTER)

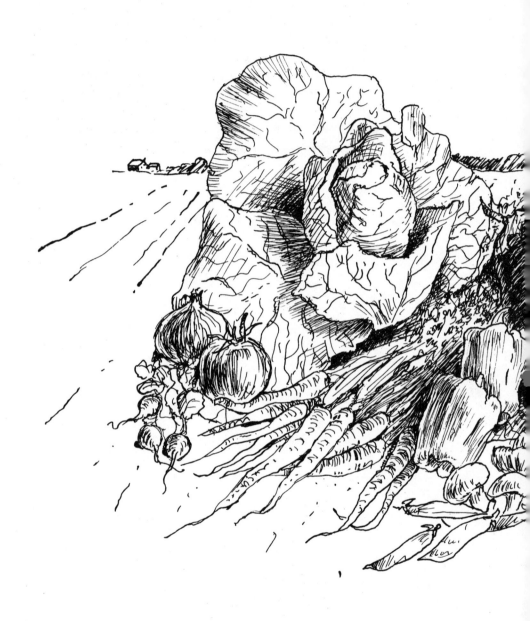

SUMMER

Artichoke Dip

8–10 fresh artichoke hearts or 1 14-ounce can
½ cup mayonnaise
Crushed garlic to taste
Sprinkling of cayenne pepper, optional
Freshly grated Parmesan cheese
Dash of paprika

Preheat the oven to 350°.

Parboil the artichoke hearts if fresh. Purée the hearts, and stir in the mayonnaise, garlic and cayenne pepper.

Pour into a baking dish, and sprinkle the cheese and paprika over the top.

Bake until hot and the cheese is melted. Serve hot or cold.

(**BARBARA MARSH**)

Artichoke Hearts Nonni

4 servings

16 fresh baby artichokes or 2 14-ounce cans
  artichoke hearts
3 tablespoons olive oil
3 cloves garlic, minced
1 teaspoon fresh marjoram
1 medium tomato, peeled, seeded and diced
2 tablespoons minced fresh Italian parsley

If you are using fresh artichokes, remove the outer tough leaves of the artichokes and cut off the tips to get to the tender hearts (it is not necessary to remove the chokes, which are edible in baby artichokes). Parboil in salted water until just tender, about 8–10 minutes.

Heat the oil in a heavy skillet over medium heat. Add the artichokes, garlic and marjoram. Stir for 1 minute and then add the tomato. Continue cooking and stirring for 1 more minute. Remove from the heat. Sprinkle with the parsley and serve.

("A family recipe from my Italian mother-in-law. When the family ate them, she'd prepare a whole sackful because no one could stop eating them."—HELEN GIAMBRUNI)

BEANS

Bean and Onion Salad
4–6 servings

2 pounds mixed yellow, green and purple string beans
1 large red Bermuda onion, thinly sliced
1 cup tarragon or red wine vinegar
Salt and freshly ground black pepper to taste
3 tablespoons virgin olive oil

Wash and trim the string beans, cut into 1-inch pieces and boil in salted water until barely tender. Plunge them into a large bowl of ice water to prevent further cooking. Remove and let cool, then drain and pat dry with paper towels.

Combine the string beans and onion in a large bowl. Add the vinegar, salt and pepper. Stir in the olive oil. Taste and adjust seasonings. Refrigerate if not to be served at once.

(JEROME ROBBINS)

Cecil B. Salad

4–6 servings

4 carrots, peeled and sliced thin on an angle
½ pound fresh green beans, trimmed and sliced thin on
  an angle
½ head broccoli, broken into flowerets
2 medium sweet red peppers, chopped
3 scallions, chopped (both white and green parts)
¼ pound pepperoni sausage, sliced
½ cup sesame oil
¼ cup white vinegar
2 teaspoons dry mustard
1 clove garlic, minced
Salt and freshly ground black pepper to taste
¼ cup sour cream, optional

Put the vegetables in a steamer for about 5 minutes, with broccoli forming the bottom layer, green beans the next layer and carrots the top layer. Immerse them in a bowl of ice water to retain their bright colors. Drain.

In a bowl, combine the cooked vegetables with the peppers, scallions and pepperoni.

Combine the remaining ingredients, pour over the vegetable salad and mix well. Chill and serve. The colors in this salad are pure Hollywood, hence the name.

(NINA COOPER)

Green Beans and Mushrooms
4–6 servings

1 pound fresh green beans, trimmed, washed and sliced
  into 2-inch lengths
½ pound fresh mushrooms
4 tablespoons butter
1½ teaspoons freshly squeezed lemon juice
2 tablespoons minced fresh parsley

Steam the green beans until crisp-tender, drain and pat dry with paper towels.

Wipe the mushrooms clean, slice and sauté quickly in a heated heavy skillet with 2 tablespoons of the butter. Add the green beans, the remaining butter and the lemon juice, and cook until the butter is melted.

Serve on a glass platter with minced parsley sprinkled on top.

(HELEN GIAMBRUNI)

Pasta della Sposa *(Bride's Pasta)*
8–10 servings

½ pound spinach pasta
½ pound tomato pasta
½ pound white pasta
½ pound green beans, steamed and cut in half
½ pound fresh peas, cooked
1 green pepper, diced
1 red pepper, diced
3 tomatoes, peeled and diced
2 cups Sorrel Mayonnaise (see page 119)
¼ pound Port Salut cheese
¼ pound Pain de Pyrénées cheese

Cook the pastas individually until they are *al dente.* Combine the cooked pastas, vegetables and mayonnaise. Mix thoroughly, cover and refrigerate for several hours.

Before serving, cut the cheeses into julienne strips and add to the pasta. Serve cold.

(THE PORTABLE EPICURE, LTD.)

Haricots Verts Fines
4 servings

1 pound thin French green beans
2 quarts boiling water
2 teaspoons salt
3 tablespoons sweet butter
Salt and freshly ground black pepper to taste
1 teaspoon freshly squeezed lemon juice

Pinch off the stem end of each bean, wash and drain. Put them in boiling water to which the 2 teaspoons of salt have been added. Boil until the beans are cooked *al dente,* about 10 minutes; do not overcook. Drain the beans in a colander. Refill the pot with cold water, place the beans in it, and when they are chilled, drain again.

Just before serving, melt the butter in a saucepan and toss the beans in it. While tossing, add salt, pepper and lemon juice. Serve warm.

(MARGOT WELLINGTON)

Mother "B's" Succotash

8 servings

¼ pound fresh salt pork
1 pound fresh lima beans, shelled
12 ears fresh corn
4 tablespoons butter
Freshly ground black pepper to taste
½ cup half-and-half, optional

Cut the salt pork in half. In a large saucepan, combine the pork and lima beans. Add enough water to cover and bring to a boil. Reduce the heat and simmer for 20 minutes. Remove from the heat and set aside. Do not drain. Shuck the corn. Run a sharp knife lengthwise down each row of kernels, halving each kernel into a bowl. Then scrape the balance of the kernels off the cob into the bowl.

Add the corn and butter to the lima beans and pork, and simmer for 7 minutes. Remove the pork. Season with the pepper. For a richer succotash, add half-and-half.

(JOHN BIDWELL)

Lima Beans and Corn

3–4 servings

2 pounds fresh lima beans, shelled
2 medium-sized ripe tomatoes, peeled and finely chopped
1 tablespoon butter
4 ears corn
Salt and freshly ground black pepper to taste

Place the lima beans, tomatoes and butter in a saucepan and gently cook until the lima beans are barely tender.

Cut the kernels off the cobs. Add the corn to the beans and continue cooking until the lima beans are tender. Season with salt and pepper.

(F. C. BROWN, JR.)

CARROTS

Carrot-Cabbage Slaw
6 servings

½ cup shredded green peppers
2 cups shredded carrots
2 cups shredded red cabbage
2 cups diced zucchini
¼ cup finely chopped onions
¼ cup chopped fresh parsley
⅓ cup mayonnaise
1 teaspoon cider vinegar
Salt and freshly ground black pepper to taste

Combine the first 6 ingredients in a large bowl. Set aside.
Combine the mayonnaise, vinegar, salt and pepper in a smaller bowl, and beat with a wire whisk until smooth. Pour the dressing over the vegetables and mix thoroughly. Cover and refrigerate until ready to serve.

(HELEN COLLINS)

Lentil Soup

10 servings

1 pound lentils
3 quarts cold water
1 tablespoon salt
Freshly ground black pepper to taste
3 cups chopped celery, including tops
3 cups sliced carrots
3 medium onions, chopped
¼ cup chopped fresh parsley
2 cups chopped tomatoes
12 ounces vegetable juice
3 slices bacon
1 tablespoon white vinegar
Dash of Worcestershire sauce
1 bay leaf
Pinch of fresh oregano
10 all-beef frankfurters, sliced, **optional**

Wash the lentils and drain. Put them in a large kettle with the cold water and salt. Cover and simmer for 45 minutes.

Add all the remaining ingredients except the frankfurters, and simmer for 30 minutes. Add the frankfurters and simmer for 30 minutes more.

("My grandmother's recipe . . ." **MRS. ALBERT CAREY**)

Chicken Crêpes à la Crème
16 7-inch crêpes

FILLING
1 pound carrots, scraped and thinly sliced
2 large onions, chopped
4 tablespoons butter
1½ pounds chicken, skinned, boned and cut
  into small pieces

CRÊPE BATTER
1½ cups milk
2 tablespoons oil
3 eggs
1½ cups all-purpose flour
Salt to taste

SAUCE
4 tablespoons butter
4 tablespoons flour
2 cups chicken broth
2 cups heavy cream
Dash of cayenne pepper
Dash of ground nutmeg

4 cups cooked rice
Fresh parsley for garnish

Preheat the oven to 375°.

In a heavy skillet, sauté the carrots and onions in the butter over medium heat until barely tender. Remove with a slotted spoon and put in a mixing bowl.

Place the chicken in the skillet and sauté, adding more butter if necessary. Mix in the carrots and onions, and set aside.

Combine all the crêpe-batter ingredients in a mixing bowl, stirring with a wire whisk. Heat a well-seasoned crêpe pan and add a thin layer of batter to cover the bottom. Cook briefly and turn. Cook the other side briefly and remove from the pan. Continue until all the batter is used.

To make the sauce, melt the butter in a saucepan over low heat. Add the flour. Slowly stir in the chicken broth. When well blended, add the cream, cayenne pepper and nutmeg.

Fill each crêpe with the chicken mixture, adding a little sauce to each one. Fold the crêpes over to enclose the filling. Arrange them in a baking dish and spoon some of the sauce over them. Cover with foil and bake for 10–15 minutes, or until piping hot.

Place the crêpes in the center of a serving dish with the rice encircling them. Pour the remaining sauce over them. Garnish with fresh parsley.

(FRAN BERGENTI)

Lemon-Ginger Carrots

4 servings

½ cup butter
1 pound carrots, scraped and shredded
¼ cup sugar
2 teaspoons grated lemon rind
1 tablespoon freshly squeezed lemon juice
1 tablespoon freshly grated ginger

Melt the butter in a heavy skillet, and add the carrots and the remaining ingredients. Cook slowly, stirring, until the sugar melts. Cover and continue cooking slowly, stirring once or twice, for about 10 minutes, or until crisp-tender.

(BARBARA SLIFKA)

Carrot Pennies with Bourbon

2–3 servings

2 cups sliced carrots
½ cup water
2 teaspoons butter
2 teaspoons brown sugar
Touch of salt
3 teaspoons brandy or bourbon

Cook the carrots in the water until tender, about 10 minutes. (Add a bit more water if necessary.) Add the remaining ingredients and mix gently. Cook for 3 minutes to blend the flavors. Serve while still warm.

(F. C. BROWN, JR.)

Dilled Carrots

4–6 servings

1 pound carrots
2 tablespoons butter
2 tablespoons white wine or dry vermouth
½ teaspoon salt
Dash of white pepper
1 tablespoon snipped fresh dill

Scrape the carrots and cut into matchstick-size pieces. Combine the carrots, butter, wine, salt and pepper in a saucepan and cook for 5–6 minutes, or until barely tender.

Sprinkle with dill, toss gently and serve.

(HELEN COLLINS)

Peggy's Carrot Pudding
8–10 servings

½ cup shortening
1 cup sugar
1½ cups grated carrots
1 cup grated raw potatoes
1 cup all-purpose flour
1 teaspoon baking soda
1 teaspoon salt
1 teaspoon ground cinnamon
½ teaspoon ground cloves
½ teaspoon ground nutmeg
1 cup raisins
½ cup chopped citron

Preheat the oven to 325°.

Cream together the shortening and sugar in a large mixing bowl. Stir in the carrots and potatoes. Set aside.

Sift together the flour, baking soda, salt, cinnamon, cloves and nutmeg. Stir this into the carrot mixture and blend well. Add the raisins and citron, mixing thoroughly.

Fill a greased pudding mold three-quarters full. Cover tightly. Steam in the oven for 2½ hours. Serve hot with hard sauce (recipe follows).

(AT EASE CATERERS)

BASIC HARD SAUCE
2 cups

8 tablespoons butter
2 cups confectioners' sugar
1 teaspoon vanilla extract

Thoroughly cream together the butter and sugar. Add the vanilla and blend. Cover and refrigerate until needed.

For variations, omit the vanilla and use 2 tablespoons of brandy, or 3 tablespoons of raspberry jam, or 1 tablespoon of freshly squeezed lemon juice and 1 tablespoon of grated lemon rind.

Carrot Cake

8 servings

2 cups all-purpose flour
2 cups sugar
2 teaspoons baking soda
2 teaspoons ground cinnamon
1½ cups oil
4 eggs, beaten
2 teaspoons vanilla extract
3 cups grated raw carrots
½ cup chopped walnuts

Preheat the oven to 350°. Grease and flour a 9 × 13-inch pan.

Sift together the flour, sugar, baking soda and cinnamon into a large mixing bowl. Slowly stir in the oil, eggs and vanilla. When thoroughly blended, stir in the carrots. Mix well and add the walnuts.

When well blended, pour into the prepared pan and bake for 40 minutes, or until a knife inserted into the center comes out clean. May be eaten plain, with fresh whipped cream, or with Cream Cheese Icing (see page 168).

(DORIS KATZ)

Wheat Germ Carrot Cake

8 servings

¾ cup wheat germ
1 cup unsifted all-purpose flour
1 cup sugar
¾ teaspoon baking soda
¾ teaspoon baking powder
1½ teaspoons ground cinnamon
¼ teaspoon ground nutmeg
¼ teaspoon ground ginger
½ cup oil
2 eggs, beaten
1 teaspoon vanilla extract
1 cup fresh pineapple, crushed with juice
1¼ cups grated carrots
½ cup chocolate chips
½ cup chopped walnuts
½ cup raisins

Preheat the oven to 350°.

Combine the first 8 ingredients in a large bowl. Stir in the oil, eggs and vanilla. Blend well.

Stir in the pineapple, then the carrots, then the chocolate chips, then the walnuts and, lastly, the raisins. Blend well.

Pour the batter into a well-greased ring mold. Bake for 45 minutes, or until a knife inserted into the center comes out clean.

(IRENE TULLY)

CORN

Corn on the Cob

Ideally, corn should be shucked and cooked within a few minutes of the time it leaves the garden. At The Green Thumb, we pick corn several times a day to ensure freshness. Corn should be refrigerated in the husk until you are ready to cook it—but never longer than absolutely necessary.

Fill a kettle with enough water to cover the corn and bring the water to a rolling boil. Shuck the ears, remove the silk and plunge the corn into the boiling water. (*Note*: Adding salt to the water tends to toughen the corn. Some people add sugar to enhance the sweetness. We use neither.)

When the water comes to a boil again, cook the corn for 3–5 minutes. Very young tender corn needs to be cooked for about 3 minutes. The shorter the cooking time, the better the corn will be.

Place the corn in a dish lined with a linen napkin to fold over it to hold in the heat. Serve with salt, pepper and butter.

Corn Chowder

14 servings

10 tablespoons butter
3 large onions, chopped
1 large red pepper, seeded and diced
8 medium potatoes, peeled and diced
5 cups milk
2 cups heavy cream
6 cups fresh corn, scraped off the cobs
¼ cup minced fresh parsley
Salt and freshly ground black pepper to taste
Freshly grated nutmeg

Melt 4 tablespoons of the butter in a heavy skillet. Add the onions and sauté until soft and transparent. Add the red pepper and sauté briefly. Remove from the heat.

Cook the potatoes in enough boiling salted water to cover until tender but still firm. Drain well.

Combine the milk and cream in a large saucepan and heat slowly. When thoroughly hot, add the onion-pepper mixture, potatoes, corn, parsley, salt, pepper and nutmeg. Simmer until well blended. Remove from the heat and let stand for several hours before serving.

Just before serving, reheat the soup and add the remaining butter, stirring gently. Delicious and filling.

Corn Miechel

2 servings

3 ears fresh corn
2–3 tablespoons butter
Salt and freshly ground black pepper to taste

Cut the kernels off the corn. (The corn can be either cooked or uncooked.)

Melt the butter in a heavy skillet over low heat. Sauté the corn until it starts to pop. Cover and continue cooking until golden brown. Season with salt and pepper. Great for breakfast!

(KAL ABRETT)

Corn-Zucchini Soufflé

6 servings

2 ears fresh corn
2–3 zucchini
2¼ teaspoons salt
6 tablespoons butter
¼ cup chopped fresh chives
6 tablespoons all-purpose flour
¼ teaspoon freshly ground black pepper
1¼ cups milk
6 eggs, separated
½ cup grated Swiss cheese

Preheat the oven to 350°. Butter a 2-quart soufflé dish.

Boil the corn until just done, drain and cut off the kernels. Set aside.

Coarsely grate the zucchini, sprinkle with 1 teaspoon of the salt and let stand in a colander for 10 minutes. Press to remove any excess liquid.

Melt 1 tablespoon of the butter in a heavy skillet, add the zucchini and sauté for 5 minutes. Stir in the chives. Remove from the heat and set aside.

Melt the remaining butter in a saucepan. Blend in the flour, the remaining salt and the pepper. Cook until bubbly, stirring with a wire whisk. Gradually add the milk and continue stirring until the mixture thickens. Remove from the heat and set aside.

Beat the egg yolks in a large bowl. Gradually add the hot butter-milk mixture. Stir in the cheese, corn and zucchini.

Beat the egg whites until soft peaks form. Fold into the corn-zucchini mixture until no white streaks remain. Pour into the soufflé dish and bake for 55 minutes, or until puffed and golden.

(ANNA NOEL)

CUCUMBERS

Cucumber Coriander

4 servings

½ cup mayonnaise
½ cup sour cream
3 tablespoons white vinegar
Sugar to taste
2 cucumbers, peeled and sliced
½ medium-sized sweet red Italian onion, thinly sliced
5 tablespoons chopped fresh coriander
Freshly ground black pepper to taste

Combine the mayonnaise, sour cream, vinegar and sugar in a medium-sized bowl. Stir in the cucumbers and onion. Blend in the coriander and pepper. Chill well. Toss before serving.

(JEAN McCLINTOCK)

Cucumber Soup I

4 servings

2 cups minced or grated peeled cucumbers
1 tablespoon salt
2 cups plain yogurt
1 clove garlic, minced
1 teaspoon vinegar
1½ tablespoons chopped fresh dill
3 tablespoons olive oil
Freshly ground black pepper to taste
Fresh mint leaves for garnish

In a bowl, sprinkle the cucumbers with the salt. Let stand for
1 hour. Then put the cucumbers in a colander or sieve, pressing out as much liquid as possible.

Whip the yogurt until smooth. Blend in the cucumber and
all the remaining ingredients except the mint leaves. Chill for
several hours.

If the soup is too thick, add a little cold chicken broth or ice
water. Spoon into chilled bowls and garnish each bowl with a
mint leaf.

(JULES BOND)

Cucumber Soup II
4–6 servings

4 small cucumbers, peeled and sliced
2 medium onions, chopped
1¼ quarts chicken broth
2 pounds potatoes, washed
2 teaspoons fresh dill
Salt and freshly ground black pepper to taste
1 teaspoon fresh rosemary
6 ounces cream cheese
1 cup heavy cream

Place the cucumbers, onions and chicken broth in a pot and simmer uncovered for about 30 minutes, or until the onion is soft and transparent.

Boil the potatoes separately. Then cool and remove the skins.

Combine all the ingredients in a food processor or blender and process until smooth. Serve chilled or at room temperature.

(C. B. PECK)

Atjar Ketimum
(Sweet and Sour Indonesian Relish)
8–10 servings

2 cucumbers, peeled and cut into paper-thin slices
Salt
½ cup white vinegar
3 tablespoons sugar
¼ cup water
1 teaspoon shaved ginger
2 cloves garlic, shaved
Pinch of red pepper flakes

Sprinkle the cucumbers lightly with salt and let stand for 20 minutes. Drain.

Combine the remaining ingredients in a saucepan and boil for 2 minutes. Remove from the heat and cool.

Add the cucumbers and let stand for several hours before serving. Serve at room temperature or chilled.

(SHELLEY MODLIN)

Bread and Butter Pickles

12–14 pints

8 pounds small cucumbers, 3 to 4 inches long
8 small onions, thinly sliced
2 green peppers, cut in strips
½ cup pickling salt
1 quart crushed ice
4½ cups sugar
5 cups cider vinegar
1½ teaspoons turmeric
½ teaspoon ground cloves
2 tablespoons mustard seed
1 teaspoon celery salt

Wash the cucumbers and cut them into paper-thin slices. Combine the cucumbers, onions, green peppers and salt. Mix with the crushed ice and let stand for 3 hours. Drain.

Combine the remaining ingredients and pour over the vegetables. Place the mixture in a saucepan and slowly bring to the boiling point, stirring occasionally. Pack in sterilized jars and seal at once.

For the best flavor, let stand at least 30 days before using.

(**PEACHIE HALSEY**)

Dill Pickles

6 quarts

20 washed cucumbers, 3 to 4 inches long
1 quart cider vinegar
3 quarts water
1 cup salt
12 sprigs flowering dill
12 cloves garlic, peeled

Place the cucumbers in a bowl and cover with cold water. Let soak overnight. Drain and wipe dry.

Combine the cider vinegar, water and salt in a saucepan and boil for 3 minutes. Remove from the heat and set aside. Place a sprig of dill and a clove of garlic in each hot, sterilized quart jar. Fill each jar with the cucumbers. Add another sprig of dill and a clove of garlic to the quart jars. Cover with the vinegar/water mixture, leaving ¼-inch head space in each jar. Seal and refrigerate, or process according to the directions on the jar.

Let stand for 6 weeks before eating.

(PEACHIE HALSEY)

EGGPLANT

Sicilian Eggplant Appetizer

8 cups

2 pounds eggplant, peeled and cut into ½-inch cubes
Salt
½ cup olive oil
2 cups finely chopped celery
¾ cup finely chopped onions
⅓ cup wine vinegar
4 teaspoons sugar
3 cups plum tomatoes, peeled
2 tablespoons tomato paste
6 large green olives, pitted and slivered
2 tablespoons capers
4 flat anchovy filets, rinsed well to remove salt and
   pounded into a paste
Salt and freshly ground black pepper to taste
2 tablespoons pine nuts

Sprinkle the eggplant cubes generously with salt and put in a colander to drain. After 30 minutes, pat the cubes dry with paper towels and set aside.

Heat ¼ cup of the oil in a heavy 12-inch skillet over moderate heat. Add the celery and cook for 10 minutes, stirring frequently. Stir in the onions and continue cooking for another 8–10 minutes, or until the celery and onions are soft and slightly browned. With a slotted spoon, transfer them to a bowl.

Pour the remaining oil into the skillet, add the eggplant cubes and sauté over high heat, stirring and turning constantly, for about 8 minutes, or until they are lightly browned.

Combine the vinegar and sugar. Return the celery and onions to the skillet and stir in the vinegar mixture, tomatoes, tomato paste, olives, capers, anchovies, salt and pepper. Bring to a boil, reduce the heat and simmer, uncovered, for about 15 minutes, stirring frequently. Stir in the pine nuts. Taste and adjust the seasonings.

Refrigerate for at least 24 hours before serving. This will keep well in the refrigerator for 2–3 weeks.

("I learned this recipe from an elderly Sicilian lady, who commented that 'if care was not taken in the kitchen, care would not be taken with any order of life.' "—NANCY WASSERMAN)

Hot Eggplant Puffs
8 servings

1 medium eggplant
½ cup grated Swiss cheese
1 egg, beaten
½ cup bread crumbs
½ teaspoon freshly squeezed lemon juice
½ teaspoon salt
¼ teaspoon white pepper
¾ teaspoon garlic powder
Oil for frying

Cook the eggplant whole in boiling salted water for 15–20 minutes, or until tender. Peel and mash. Set aside.

Combine the cheese, egg, ¼ cup of the bread crumbs and the lemon juice, salt, pepper and garlic. Mix thoroughly. Stir in the mashed eggplant. Blend well, cover and refrigerate for 1 hour.

Shape into balls, roll in the remaining bread crumbs and deep-fry. Drain and serve.

(JANICE LORD)

Baby Eggplant Salad
4–6 servings

1 pound baby eggplants, unpeeled
1 clove garlic
1 teaspoon paprika
1 teaspoon cumin
2 tablespoons freshly squeezed lemon juice
1 tablespoon olive oil
1 handful chopped fresh parsley

Cut the eggplants in quarters lengthwise. Cook with the garlic in boiling salted water until the eggplant is tender. Drain and discard the garlic.

Combine the remaining ingredients and mix gently with the eggplant. Chill before serving.

(MARION PORTER)

Harmon Rat-Tat

4 servings

1 medium eggplant, unpeeled and diced
1 medium zucchini, sliced
5 ripe tomatoes, cut into chunks
1 small can black olives, pitted and halved
5 sausage links, sliced, optional
1 yellow summer squash, sliced
1 cup fresh mushrooms, sliced
6 garlic cloves, finely minced
3 tablespoons olive oil
Salt and freshly ground black pepper to taste

Preheat the oven to 350°.

Combine the first 8 ingredients and place in a large oiled roasting pan. Sprinkle with the oil, cover and bake for 1½–2 hours, stirring occasionally. Season with salt and pepper.

Rat-Tat may be served hot or cold as a side dish or an hors d'oeuvre. It can also be used as a filling for omelets.

(MARIAN HARMON)

Eggplant Rollups

6 servings

2 medium eggplants, unpeeled
1½ cups ricotta or cottage cheese
¼ cup freshly grated Parmesan cheese
1 tablespoon finely chopped fresh basil
Salt and freshly ground black pepper to taste
2 cups marinara sauce
4–6 ounces mozzarella cheese, cut into thin slices

Preheat the oven to 375°.

Slice the eggplants lengthwise into 8–12 slices, each slice ½ inch thick. Place them in a lightly greased baking pan and bake for 35 minutes, or until somewhat brown. Cool.

Combine the cheeses, basil, salt and pepper in a mixing bowl. Place 2–3 tablespoons of the mixture in the center of each eggplant slice and roll each one, jelly-roll-style, starting at the narrow end.

Cover the bottom of a 9 × 13-inch baking pan with a small amount of marinara sauce. Put the rollups seam side down in the pan and pour the remaining marinara sauce over them. Place the mozzarella cheese on top of the rollups.

Reduce oven temperature to 350° and bake for 25 minutes, or until bubbly. Serve with additional grated Parmesan cheese.

This dish can be made in advance and reheated. Serve with a tossed green salad and French bread.

(JOAN T. CARLSON)

Eggplant-Stuffed Chicken
4–6 servings

4 tablespoons butter
1 medium onion, finely chopped
1 large red pepper, finely chopped
2 stalks celery, finely chopped
½ cup finely chopped fresh parsley
1 medium eggplant, peeled and finely chopped
Salt and freshly ground black pepper to taste
1 slice toast, broken into small pieces
1 roasting chicken (4½–5 pounds)
¼ pound butter, softened
Sprinkling of salt, pepper and paprika

Preheat the oven to 325°.

Melt the butter in a heavy skillet and sauté the onion, pepper, celery and parsley until the onion is transparent.

Add the eggplant and continue cooking until the eggplant is soft, about 10 more minutes, stirring frequently. Season with salt and pepper. Add the toast pieces and mix well.

Rinse the chicken and pat dry. Stuff with the eggplant mixture. Rub the butter all over the chicken and sprinkle with salt, pepper and paprika.

Place the chicken on a V-shaped rack in a roasting pan and bake, basting every 15 minutes with the pan drippings. Cook about 25 minutes per pound. Remove from the oven and let stand for 10 minutes before carving.

(BERNICE SCHWARTZ)

Rice Provençale

6 servings

1 cup diced unpeeled baby eggplants
1 cup diced zucchini
Salt
1 cup sliced white mushrooms
1 teaspoon freshly squeezed lemon juice
2 tablespoons imported olive oil
¼ cup diced green peppers
¼ cup diced sweet red peppers
1 tablespoon minced garlic
1 cup chopped peeled and seeded tomatoes
Salt and freshly ground black pepper to taste
2 tablespoons butter
2 tablespoons finely chopped onions
1 cup uncooked rice
1½ cups chicken broth
1 sprig fresh thyme

Place the eggplant and zucchini in a colander, sprinkle with salt and allow to drain for 30 minutes, tossing occasionally. Place on paper towels and pat dry.

Toss the mushrooms with the lemon juice.

Heat the olive oil in a heavy saucepan over medium heat and stir in the eggplant, zucchini, mushrooms, green and red peppers, and garlic. Sauté until soft; do not brown. Add the tomatoes and stir just long enough to warm. Season with salt and black pepper. Remove from the heat and set aside.

Melt the butter in a 1½-quart saucepan over low heat. Add the onions and sauté until soft. Add the rice and stir to coat with the butter mixture. Add the chicken broth and thyme and bring to a boil; cover and simmer for 17 minutes, or until all the water is absorbed.

Using two forks, toss the rice and vegetables together and place in a pretty serving dish.

(HELEN GREEN)

Broiled Eggplant Slices

4 servings

2 medium eggplants, unpeeled
2 cloves garlic
1 tablespoon salt
1 teaspoon shredded fresh oregano,
  or ¼ teaspoon dried oregano
⅓ cup olive oil
1 tablespoon red wine vinegar

Slice each eggplant into ½-inch slices. Crush the garlic with the salt and the remaining ingredients, and mix well.

Brush each eggplant slice with the mixture and broil at medium heat until tender and brown on both sides. Baste with leftover mixture several times while broiling.

("This recipe came from my aunt, who made me a homemade cookbook that included all her favorite recipes."—JOANNE LEHU)

Eggplant Curry

6 servings

2 eggplants
5 tablespoons imported olive oil
Grated fresh ginger to taste
2 cloves garlic, minced
1 medium onion, finely chopped
1 tablespoon turmeric
2 teaspoons ground cumin
1 teaspoon finely chopped fresh coriander
½ fresh chili pepper, seeded and finely chopped
2 cups chopped tomatoes
Dash of cinnamon, nutmeg and freshly ground black
   pepper
Fresh parsley, raisins and almonds for garnish

Broil the eggplants whole by making gashes in them and setting them under the flame. In about 15 minutes, the eggplants
will "collapse" and express liquid. Turn once and broil for a
few minutes more. Let cool. Remove the outer layer of skin
and finely chop the eggplants.

In a large, heavy skillet, heat the oil over low heat and sauté
the ginger, garlic and onion. When the onion is soft and transparent, add the turmeric, cumin, coriander and chili pepper.
Stir until well blended, and then add the tomatoes and eggplants. Simmer uncovered for 15 minutes.

Sprinkle with cinnamon, nutmeg and pepper, and mix well.
Garnish with parsley, raisins and almonds. Serve with Date
and Lemon Chutney (page 90).

(**MAGGIE JOFFE**)

ENDIVE

Endive and Walnut Salad

2 servings

2 heads Belgian endive, quartered lengthwise
¼ cup coarsely chopped walnuts
2 tablespoons walnut oil
1 tablespoon freshly squeezed lemon juice
Salt and freshly ground black pepper to taste

Divide the endive evenly between 2 salad plates. Sprinkle with the walnuts. Mix together the oil, lemon juice, salt and pepper. Pour the dressing over the endive.

Endive and Watercress Salad

4 servings

5 heads endive, cored and separated into leaves
1 bunch watercress, stems removed
4 small beets, washed, peeled and shredded
2 cloves garlic
¼ cup oil
2 tablespoons imported prepared mustard, such as Dijon
2 tablespoons vinegar
Salt and freshly ground black pepper to taste

Arrange the endive leaves around the edge of a salad bowl. Mound the watercress in the center. Arrange the beets between the two in a circular fashion.

Combine the remaining ingredients in a blender or food processor and process until smooth. Taste and adjust seasonings. Drizzle over the salad and serve.

Pasta Salad

8 servings

1 pound fresh pasta
4 heads Belgian endive, cut into ½-inch-wide pieces
1 bunch watercress, chopped
4 scallions, chopped (green and white parts)
½ pound mushrooms, sliced
2 medium-sized ripe tomatoes, seeded and chopped
1 green pepper, chopped
2 small golden zucchini, chopped
1 clove garlic, minced
½ cup freshly grated imported Parmesan cheese
¼ cup olive oil
Juice of 1 lemon
1 cup chopped fresh parsley
Salt and freshly ground black pepper to taste
Pine nuts or pistachio nuts, **optional**

Cook the pasta until the desired degree of doneness. Drain and run cold water on it to stop the cooking process. Combine all the ingredients in a large bowl and mix thoroughly.

(ALISON MARTIN)

SUMMER FRUITS

Waldorf Chicken with Curry
8–10 servings

6 chicken cutlets, skinned and boned
3 stalks celery, diced
1 medium onion, diced
2 medium apples, cut into bite-sized pieces
Small bunch seedless grapes, halved
1 cup mayonnaise or yogurt
2 teaspoons curry powder
1 cup broken walnut pieces
Large leaves of red cabbage, optional

Broil the chicken cutlets. (For added flavor, brush the chicken with a vinaigrette dressing before cooking.) Cool and cut into chunky pieces.

Add the celery, onion, apples and grapes, and mix well.

Combine the mayonnaise and curry powder and stir into the chicken mixture. Add the walnuts. Chill in the refrigerator. For added color, serve on a bed of large red cabbage leaves.

(MARIAN SALTZMAN)

Fresh Banana Whip

2 servings

13 ounces (about 3 medium-large) very ripe
  bananas, peeled
Juice of 1 lemon
½ cup milk

Brush the bananas with the lemon juice to prevent discoloration. Wrap them in aluminum foil, place in the freezer and let
stand for at least 24 hours. Remove the bananas from the
freezer and slice thinly.

Pour the milk into a blender container, add about two thirds
of the banana slices and blend on high speed, stopping the
motor to push the unblended slices into the blender blades. Be
sure the blades have stopped rotating before attempting this
step. Add the remaining slices and process until thoroughly
blended. The resulting product will have the consistency and
flavor of soft banana ice cream. Serve immediately.

(VICTORIA DOLCIMASCOLO)

Banana Nut Bread

2 loaves

1 teaspoon freshly squeezed lemon juice
½ cup milk
1 cup sweet butter, softened
2½ cups sugar
2 teaspoons vanilla extract
4 eggs, beaten
3½ cups unsifted unbleached flour
2 teaspoons baking soda
¼ teaspoon salt
2½ cups mashed very ripe bananas
2 cups chopped walnuts

Preheat the oven to 350°. Butter 2 loaf pans.

Pour the lemon juice into the milk and stir until the milk is curdled. Set aside.

Beat together the butter, sugar and vanilla until creamy. Add the eggs, mixing thoroughly.

Sift together the flour, baking soda and salt, and add to the butter-sugar mixture alternately with the curdled milk. Stir in the bananas and nuts.

Pour the batter into the prepared loaf pans and bake for 1 hour and 10 minutes, or until a knife inserted into the center comes out clean.

("My great-grandmother won first prize with this recipe at the Wabash, Indiana, County Fair in 1889, and all her great-grandchildren subsequently grew up on it."—MARCY OLIVE)

Banana Bran Muffins

12–20 muffins, depending on size of muffin tins

¼ pound sweet butter
1 cup sugar
3 eggs, beaten
1 cup bran cereal
1 heaping cup mashed ripe bananas
¼ cup buttermilk
1¾ cups all-purpose flour
1½ teaspoons baking powder
½ teaspoon baking soda
½ teaspoon salt

Preheat the oven to 350°.

Cream together the butter and sugar. Stir in the eggs.

In a separate bowl, combine the bran cereal, bananas and buttermilk. When thoroughly blended, stir into the egg mixture.

Sift together the flour, baking powder, baking soda and salt, and fold into the banana mixture.

Fill ungreased muffin tins two-thirds full and bake for 25 minutes.

(MRS. SAMUEL SWINT)

Green Thumb
"Special Banana" Bread
1 loaf

1¾ cups all-purpose flour
2 teaspoons baking powder
¼ teaspoon baking soda
½ teaspoon salt
⅓ cup shortening, softened
⅔ cup sugar
2 eggs, beaten
1 cup mashed bananas
1 cup raisins
1 cup chocolate chips
¼ cup chocolate syrup

Preheat the oven to 350°. Grease and flour a 9 × 5 × 3-inch loaf pan.

Sift together the first 4 ingredients. Set aside.

In a large mixing bowl, cream together the shortening and sugar. Stir in the eggs, blending thoroughly. Fold in bananas. Slowly stir in the flour mixture. When thoroughly blended, stir in the raisins and chocolate chips.

Pour into the prepared pan. Drizzle chocolate syrup over the top and then swirl a knife through it to create a marbling effect.

Bake for 1 hour, or until a knife inserted into the center comes out clean. Cool in the pan for 10 minutes, then remove. Best served warm with butter.

(When the bananas are very ripe at The Green Thumb, they are placed in a basket and sold as "special bananas" at a lower price—they are wonderful for baking!)

(DIANA CONKLIN)

Blueberry Crumb Cake

9 servings

CAKE

½ cup sweet butter
¾ cup sugar
1 egg, beaten
2 cups all-purpose flour
2 teaspoons baking powder
½ teaspoon salt
½ cup milk
2 cups fresh blueberries

TOPPING

¼ cup butter, softened
½ cup sugar
⅓ cup flour
½ teaspoon ground cinnamon

Preheat the oven to 375°.

Cream together the butter and sugar. Blend in the egg.

Sift together the flour, baking powder and salt. Add the flour mixture alternately with the milk to the butter mixture. Beat until smooth. Gradually fold in the blueberries. Pour into an ungreased 9 × 9 × 2-inch pan.

To make the topping, combine all the ingredients. Sprinkle over the cake. Bake for 35 minutes.

Variation: Add ½ teaspoon of grated lemon peel and 1–2 tablespoons of lemon juice to the cake batter.

(LYN ROSENBLATT)

Blueberry Kuchen
6–8 servings

1 cup plus 2 tablespoons all-purpose flour, sifted
Pinch of salt
1 cup plus 2 tablespoons sugar
½ cup butter, softened
1 tablespoon white vinegar
Dash of ground cinnamon
3 cups blueberries
Confectioners' sugar

Preheat the oven to 400°.

Combine 1 cup of the flour, the salt and 2 tablespoons of the sugar in a mixing bowl. Cut in the butter with a pastry blender. Mix in the vinegar. Spread the mixture in a 9-inch round loose-bottomed pan, ¼ inch deep and 1 inch high around the sides.

Combine 1 cup of the sugar, 2 tablespoons of the flour, and the cinnamon in a mixing bowl. Gently stir in 2 cups of the blueberries. Pour into the pan and bake for 50–60 minutes, or until the custard is set and the edges are light brown.

Remove from the oven and sprinkle with the remaining blueberries. Cool, then remove from the pan. Dust with confectioners' sugar.

(MRS. HERBERT WHEELER)

Lemon Marinade

1 ½ cups

½ cup soy sauce
½ cup freshly squeezed lemon juice
½ cup salad oil
½ teaspoon freshly ground black pepper
2 bay leaves
2 cloves garlic, crushed
2 whole cloves
½ teaspoon fresh thyme
½ teaspoon fresh oregano

Combine all the ingredients and mix well. This can be used on lamb, which should be marinated at least overnight. Drain well before cooking.

(GENE BOUCHER)

Date and Lemon Chutney

6 servings

1 cup dates, pitted
¼ cup freshly squeezed lemon juice
2 tablespoons finely minced fresh ginger
½ teaspoon fennel seeds
Salt and freshly ground black pepper to taste
1 4-inch square of fresh coconut, grated

Mash the dates with the lemon juice and ginger in a mixing bowl.

Bruise the fennel seeds by rubbing between your palms, then add them to the mixture. Season with salt and pepper. Stir in the coconut. Serve at once, or refrigerate for 2–3 days. Chutney is delicious with Eggplant Curry (see page 80) or with cucumbers and yogurt.

(MAGGIE JOFFE)

Lemon Crème

6 servings

1 envelope unflavored gelatin
½ cup freshly squeezed lemon juice
6 eggs, separated
¾ cup sugar or less, depending on individual taste
1 pint heavy cream

In a small saucepan, melt the gelatin in the lemon juice over low heat. Let cool, then stir in the egg yolks and sugar.

Beat the heavy cream until thick and add to the lemon mixture. Beat the egg whites until stiff and carefully fold into the lemon-cream mixture. Chill before serving.

(MARIANNE STEINER)

Lime Barbecued Chicken
4 servings

Juice of 3 limes
2 cloves garlic, finely chopped
1 small fresh gingerroot, finely chopped
6 tablespoons tamari or soy sauce
3 tablespoons fresh rosemary or thyme
3 tablespoons olive oil
2 whole chicken breasts, split in half

Combine the first 6 ingredients in an electric blender or food processor. Blend well. Pour the sauce over the chicken and marinate for at least 4 hours.

Cook the chicken on a slowish grill for about 30 minutes, turning once. Be careful not to char the outside of the chicken too rapidly.

(PATRICIA ZOHN)

Cream of Mango with Kiwi
2 servings

1 ripe mango
½ cup freshly squeezed orange juice
1 tablespoon Grand Marnier
1 firm ripe kiwi

Peel the mango and remove the pit. Blend the pulp with the orange juice in a blender or food processor until smooth. Stir in the Grand Marnier. Pour into individual dessert dishes and chill.

Peel the kiwi and slice horizontally. Decorate the mango cream with kiwi before serving.

(BARBARA SOBOTKA MARSH)

Mango Smash
2 servings

1 medium very ripe mango, peeled and cubed
¾ cup ice-cold skim milk
1½ teaspoons vanilla extract
2 ice cubes
Honey to taste

Put all the ingredients in a blender or food processor and blend until the sound of the ice grinding is finished. The result should be very thick and creamy but pourable.

(ENID ROTHENBERG)

Fruit Salad Andalusia

6 servings

2 navel oranges, peeled and diced
1 large apple, peeled and diced
1 cup whole seedless grapes
1–2 ripe peaches, peeled and diced
1 cup fresh strawberries, washed, hulled and sliced
1 banana, sliced
1 lemon
Sugar to taste
¾ cup freshly squeezed orange juice
1 tablespoon freshly squeezed lemon juice
1 tablespoon Triple Sec, optional

Combine the first 6 ingredients in a large bowl, adding seasonal and exotic fruits, such as mango and kiwi. Set aside.

Grate the zest from the lemon. Mash the sugar and lemon zest together using a heavy spoon. Add the juices and Triple Sec, and blend well. Pour the sauce over the fruit and mix well.

Chill for at least 30 minutes before serving.

The fruits can be varied, but all must be fresh. As the season changes, so do the fruits, but the sauce remains the same.

(CHUCK COHEN)

Orange Cake

1 cup sweet butter
2¾ cups sugar
3 whole eggs, beaten
3 cups flour
1½ teaspoons baking soda
1½ teaspoons salt
1 cup buttermilk
1 cup plus 1 tablespoon freshly squeezed orange juice
Grated rind of 1 orange
1 cup chopped dates
1 cup chopped nuts

Preheat the oven to 350°. Grease and flour an angel-food pan.

Cream together the butter and 1¾ cups of the sugar. Blend in the eggs.

Sift together the flour, baking soda and salt. Add to the butter mixture alternately with the buttermilk. Stir in 1 tablespoon of the orange juice.

When the batter is thoroughly blended, stir in one half of the grated orange rind and all the chopped dates and nuts. Pour into the prepared pan and bake for 1 hour and 10 minutes, checking after 1 hour (the cake is done when a knife inserted into the center comes out clean).

Combine the remaining sugar, orange juice and orange rind and pour over the warm cake. Let the cake stand for 2 days before serving.

(MRS. MARGARET THIELE)

Peach Chutney

11 pints

4 pounds peaches
2 pounds tart apples
1 bunch celery
2 15-ounce boxes seedless raisins
8 cups sugar
6 cups cider vinegar
4 teaspoons salt
2 red peppers, diced
2 green peppers, diced
1 pound pecan nuts, broken

Peel the peaches, remove the pits and chop. Peel, core and chop the apples. Dice the celery. Steam the raisins for 5 minutes, then drain thoroughly.

Combine the peaches, apples, sugar, vinegar, salt and peppers in a large, heavy saucepan. Boil gently until clear and slightly thick, stirring occasionally. Add the celery, raisins and nuts, and cook for 5 minutes longer. Pour into hot sterilized jars and seal.

(MRS. CHARLOTTE LAUBE)

Fruits Flambé

6 servings

1 tablespoon sweet butter
3 very ripe peaches, peeled and sliced
3 very ripe bananas, peeled and sliced
½ cup Cointreau
¼ cup Grand Marnier
1 quart vanilla ice cream

Melt the butter in a chafing dish. Add the fruits and Cointreau, and let cook until the fruits are very hot. Stir in the Grand Marnier and let it, too, become very hot.

To ignite, put additional Grand Mariner into a chafing spoon or any large spoon. Hold the spoon over the chafing-dish flame until the liqueur ignites, then pour it onto the fruits, and *voilà —flambé!*

Spoon over ice cream balls in individual dishes while still warm.

(JACKSON GRAY)

Fresh Peaches Amaretto
di Saronno

6 servings

6 firm ripe peaches
1 cup crushed Amaretto di Saronno cookies
2 tablespoons sugar
4 tablespoons sweet butter, softened
2 egg yolks

Preheat the oven to 375°. Butter an 8 × 10-inch baking dish.

Blanch the peaches, one at a time, in boiling water for about 20 seconds. Lift each peach out of the water with a slotted spoon, plunge into cold water and peel off the skin with a sharp knife. Cut the peaches in half and remove the pits. Carefully scoop out enough pulp to make a fairly deep depression in the center of each peach half. Add the pulp to the crushed cookies. Stir in the sugar, butter and egg yolks.

Stuff the peach halves with the cookie mixture. Arrange them side by side in the prepared baking dish. Bake, basting with the syrup from the pan, for about 20 minutes, or until tender. May be served hot or cold.

(NANCY WASSERMAN)

Peach Perfection

4 servings

8 ripe peaches, peeled and sliced
½ cup pure maple syrup
½ cup Frangelico liqueur

Combine all the ingredients and chill in the refrigerator for 2 hours, turning occasionally. Serve in glass bowls.

(JEAN McCLINTOCK)

Peach "Pudding"

4 servings

3–4 ripe peaches
2 eggs
8 ounces ricotta cheese
½ cup sugar
¼ teaspoon salt
¾ teaspoon vanilla extract
¼ teaspoon almond extract
Chopped walnuts, optional

Preheat the oven to 350°. Grease an 8-inch round pan.

Peel and slice the peaches. Set aside. Beat the eggs and stir in the cheese, sugar and salt. Mix until smooth. Add the vanilla and almond extracts, and blend thoroughly.

Pour the cheese mixture into the prepared pan. Arrange the sliced peaches on top. Place the pan in a larger pan of warm water and bake for 45 minutes, or until a knife inserted into the center comes out clean. Excellent served warm.

(SUSANNAH SHOPSIN)

Fruit Soup

4–6 servings

1 cup water
¼ cup sugar
1 vanilla bean, or 1 tablespoon vanilla extract
1 large McIntosh apple
1 cup freshly squeezed grapefruit juice
½ ripe pineapple
1 fresh pear or a can of mirabelle plums
1 banana
1 teaspoon almond extract

In a saucepan, heat the water, sugar and vanilla bean. Bring to a boil and simmer gently for 20 minutes, then let steep for 30 minutes. Set aside to cool.

Leaving the peel on the apple, cut the apple into quarters, core it and slice each quarter thinly. Put the slices in a large bowl and add the grapefruit juice.

Peel the pineapple and remove the eyes. Cut the pineapple lengthwise into halves, then slice into strips lengthwise. Remove any hard pith from the center of each strip. Cut the strips crosswise into thin slices and add to the apple slices.

Leaving the peel on the pear, cut the pear into quarters, core it and slice thinly in the same manner as the apple. Add to the pineapple and apple slices. (If using mirabelles, add now.)

Peel and thinly slice the banana. Add to the rest of the fruits, along with the almond extract and the sugar syrup, removing the vanilla bean. The mixture should be about one half fruit and one half syrup. Spoon into glass bowls and serve.

("This fruit salad is inspired by the *Soupe aux Fruites Exotiques* served at L'Archestrate in Paris, a three-star restaurant. Paper-thin slices of fruit float in a liquid subtly flavored to enhance and enrich the blend of fruits. It is a dessert that is satisfying yet not filling."—**DANA JACOBI**)

Plum Kuchen
6 servings

PASTRY
1 cup all-purpose flour
Pinch of salt
2 tablespoons sugar
½ cup sweet butter, softened
1 tablespoon white vinegar

FILLING
½ cup sugar
2 tablespoons flour
Dash of ground cinnamon
1½ pounds small Italian purple plums, halved and pitted

Preheat the oven to 400°.

To make the pastry, combine the flour, salt and sugar in a mixing bowl. Cut in the butter. When thoroughly blended, add the vinegar to bind. Press into an 8- or 9-inch springform pan or into a baking pan with a removable bottom.

To prepare the filling, combine the sugar, flour and cinnamon in a mixing bowl. Add the plums and stir until well coated. Place the plums cut side up on the pastry, starting with the outside ring and working toward the center. Bake for 50 minutes. Cool and remove sides of pan before serving.

(MYRA SOBEL)

Summer Fruit Tart

8 servings

PASTRY

1 cup all-purpose flour
½ cup sweet butter, softened
1 tablespoon sugar
1 egg yolk
1 tablespoon cold water

3 tablespoons rice

FILLING

2 cups milk
4 egg yolks
6 tablespoons sugar
6 tablespoons flour
1 teaspoon cornstarch
1 teaspoon butter
1 tablespoon Grand Marnier

1 pint fresh raspberries or other fruit
Confectioners' sugar

Preheat the oven to 425°.

To make the pastry, put the flour in a mixing bowl. Make a well in the center and add the butter, sugar, egg yolk and cold water. Mix with your hands until a smooth paste is formed, shape into a ball and chill, covered, for 1 hour.

Roll out the chilled dough and fit into a 9-inch flan pan with a removable bottom. Flute the edges. Cover the dough with waxed paper, place the rice on top of the paper to weight it and bake for 15 minutes. Remove the rice and waxed paper. Cool.

Reduce the oven to 350°.

To prepare the filling, scald the milk. In another saucepan, mix the egg yolks, sugar, flour and cornstarch. Slowly add the milk, stirring until thick and smooth. Cook over low heat about 45 minutes, stirring occasionally. Let cool and dot with the butter, stirring occasionally. Add the Grand Marnier and blend thoroughly.

Pour the filling into the pastry shell and bake for 20 minutes. Top with fresh raspberries or any seasonal fruit while still warm.

Sift confectioners' sugar over the top and serve at room temperature.

(PAIGE NAGLE)

Chilled Chocolate Raspberry Cake

6 servings

½ pound sweet chocolate
3 tablespoons boiling water
4 eggs, separated
4 tablespoons confectioners' sugar
9 double ladyfingers
Fresh whipped cream
1 pint fresh raspberries

Melt the chocolate in a double boiler. Add the water and blend.

Remove from the heat, add the egg yolks and beat vigorously with a whisk until smooth. Add the sugar and mix well.

Beat the egg whites until stiff and fold into the chocolate mixture.

Line the bottom and sides of an 8 × 4-inch loaf pan with waxed paper. Separate the ladyfingers and arrange 7 on the bottom and sides of the pan. Pour in the chocolate mixture. Arrange the 2 remaining ladyfingers on top.

Chill for 12–24 hours. Unmold, slice and top with whipped cream and raspberries.

(FRAN LONERGAN ANDREWS)

Raspberry Mousseline
6 servings

1 quart fresh raspberries
¾ cup sugar
1 tablespoon freshly squeezed lemon juice
2 tablespoons unflavored gelatin
¼ cup cold water
¼ cup dry white wine
½ teaspoon vanilla extract
3 tablespoons kirsch, optional
1½ cups heavy cream, whipped
1 3-ounce package ladyfingers, split

Press the raspberries through a fine sieve into a bowl to remove the seeds. Combine the purée with the sugar and lemon juice, stirring until the sugar has dissolved.

Soften the gelatin in the ¼ cup of water. Place in a small pan, add the wine and heat gently, stirring constantly, until the gelatin is dissolved. Add to the raspberry purée. Stir in the vanilla extract and kirsch. Place the bowl with the raspberry mixture in crushed ice. Stir until the purée starts to thicken. Fold in the whipped cream.

Rinse a 1½-quart mold with cold water and line the sides with the ladyfingers. Spoon the purée into the mold and chill for several hours, until well set. Turn out onto a well-chilled plate, and garnish with a few whole berries and more whipped cream, if desired.

(JULES BOND)

Raspberry Sherbet

Approximately 1 quart

1 quart fresh raspberries
¾ cup sugar
1 cup water
1 ripe banana
½ cup freshly squeezed lemon juice
2 egg whites, beaten

Boil the raspberries with the sugar and water for about 5 minutes. Put through a strainer to remove the seeds.

Purée the banana in a blender or food processor and add the lemon juice. When the raspberry syrup is cool, add the banana and lemon juice. Freeze until mushy (several hours). Remove from the freezer and stir in the egg whites. Freeze for a few more hours. Stir again before serving.

(MRS. B. J. DARNEILLE)

Raspberry Vinegar

1 quart

1 quart red wine vinegar
2 cups ripe fresh raspberries
Zest of ½ lemon, in large pieces
Juice of 1 lemon

Pour the vinegar into a 2-quart sterilized bottle. Add the raspberries, lemon zest and lemon juice. Seal the bottle and shake slightly. Store for 2–3 weeks. Strain through cheesecloth, squeezing out the berries. Replace liquid in the bottle, add a few berries for color and store in a cool, dark, dry place.

(MELISSA HALSEY)

HERBS AND SPICES

Chicken Salad Pesto
4 servings

2 whole chicken breasts
1 cup white wine
1 medium onion, sliced
6 peppercorns
½ carrot
¼ cup Romano cheese
3 cloves garlic
¼ cup walnuts
2 cups fresh basil leaves
⅓ cup oil (mix olive oil with sesame oil or
   use all olive oil)
Salt and freshly ground black pepper to taste
Boston or romaine lettuce

Poach the chicken breasts in the wine with the onion, peppercorns and carrot. Cook, covered, over medium heat for about 10 minutes, or until tender when pricked with a fork. Let the chicken cool in the broth, then remove from the saucepan. Skin and cut into large chunks. Set aside.

Process the cheese in a blender or food processor. Add the garlic, walnuts, basil, oil, salt and pepper to the cheese and continue to process until smooth.

Combine the pesto with the chicken chunks. Serve on a bed of Boston or romaine lettuce.

(JANET LAIB)

Basil Soup

8 servings

2 tablespoons butter
1 onion, sliced
4 cups fresh basil leaves
6 cups chicken broth
1 potato, diced
1 cup heavy cream
Salt and freshly ground black pepper to taste
8 fresh basil leaves for garnish

Melt the butter in a large saucepan over low heat. Add the onion and sauté until soft and transparent.

Add the 4 cups of basil leaves and cook until the leaves are wilted. Add the chicken broth and bring to a boil. Stir in the potato and continue to boil over low heat until the potato is cooked, about 5 minutes. Remove from the heat.

Pour the soup into a food processor or blender and process until smooth. Cool. Stir in the cream, salt and pepper. Spoon into individual soup bowls and garnish each bowl with a basil leaf.

(ROBERT SIMMONS, CHEF FOR AMBASSADOR AND MRS. JAMES CROMWELL)

Spaghetti with Purple Pesto
4–6 servings

2 cups purple basil leaves, washed and coarsely chopped
3 cloves garlic
½ cup pignoli nuts
½ cup freshly grated Parmesan cheese
½ cup olive oil
3 quarts water
1 pound vermicelli
½ teaspoon salt

Put the first 5 ingredients in a blender or food processor and process until smooth. (This pesto will keep a week in the refrigerator or 6 months in the freezer.)

Bring 3 quarts of water to a boil, add the vermicelli and salt. Cook until it is *al dente.* Drain well and return to the pot. Add the pesto and toss well.

(STEVEN PHILIPS)

Creamy Basil Dressing

1 cup fresh basil leaves
1 cup mayonnaise
½ cup sour cream
2 tablespoons chopped fresh parsley
3 tablespoons chopped scallions (green and white parts)
2 tablespoons wine vinegar
1 teaspoon Worcestershire sauce
Black pepper to taste
1 clove garlic

Place all the ingredients in a blender or food processor and process until thoroughly blended. Chill to thicken. Serve on tomato salad, or use as a vegetable dip.

(JACKIE LITTLE)

Basil-Dill Sauce
6 servings

2 ounces fresh Parmesan cheese, grated
4 cups loosely packed fresh basil leaves
2 tablespoons chopped fresh dill
1 clove garlic, chopped
Salt and freshly ground black pepper to taste
½ cup olive oil
1 ounce pignoli nuts

Put the cheese, basil, dill, garlic, salt and pepper in a blender or food processor. Process for approximately 10 seconds while adding ¼ cup of the oil. Add the nuts and process again while slowly adding the rest of the olive oil. Don't overprocess; the mixture should be somewhat coarse.

This is a wonderful sauce for freshly steamed green beans.

(AMY SULLIVAN)

Pesto

8 servings

2 cloves garlic, halved
1 cup loosely packed fresh basil leaves
1 cup loosely packed fresh parsley leaves
½ cup imported olive oil
⅓ cup pine nuts or walnuts
⅛ teaspoon hot pepper flakes
¾ cup freshly grated Parmesan cheese
Salt and freshly ground black pepper to taste

Combine the first 4 ingredients in a blender or food processor. Process until puréed. Add the remaining ingredients and continue to purée. Pesto tastes great on pasta and fish.

("This recipe was in my cousin's husband's family for about three generations or more—they brought it over from Italy." **—BETTY LEVINSON**)

Avocado-Chervil Salad

6 servings

4 avocados
½ cup freshly squeezed lemon juice
½ cup minced red onions
1 heaping tablespoon fresh chervil
Salt and freshly ground black pepper to taste
Boston lettuce leaves
Cherry tomatoes for garnish

Halve the avocados and remove the pits. Peel off the skin and cut the flesh into thin slices.

Combine the lemon juice, onions, chervil, salt and pepper. Arrange the avocado slices on a bed of lettuce and pour the sauce over it. Garnish with cherry tomatoes.

Epstein Fish

2 servings

1 pound striped bass filet
¼ cup virgin olive oil
Juice of 1 lemon
½ cup tightly packed chopped fresh coriander leaves
Salt and white pepper to taste
½ cup small imported black olives for garnish

Poach the bass until it becomes opaque, but no longer, about 4½–6 minutes. Drain and cool.

When it is cool enough to handle, remove and discard the skin and brown parts of the fish. Crumble the fish to the texture of lump crabmeat. Drain again.

Add the olive oil and lemon juice, and toss. Drain any excess liquid. Mix the coriander leaves into the fish and season with salt and pepper. Garnish with the olives. Serve warm as a first course at dinner or as a main course at lunch.

(JASON EPSTEIN)

Spicy Yogurt Soup

2 servings

1 cup fresh mint leaves
½ cup fresh coriander leaves
1 large garlic clove
1 fresh chili pepper
3 tablespoons freshly squeezed lime juice
1 pint plain yogurt
½ cup chopped scallions (both green and white parts)
Salt to taste
1 large cucumber, peeled, seeded and cut into ¼-inch
*   slices*

Combine ½ cup of the mint leaves and all the remaining ingredients except the cucumber in a food processor and process with the cutting blade until smooth. Chill until ready to serve.

Add the cucumber just before serving. Top each serving bowl with some of the remaining mint, if desired.

(DANA JACOBI)

Thai-Style Dip

2 cloves garlic, minced
½ medium onion, chopped
½ teaspoon hot pepper flakes
Juice of ½ lemon
1 teaspoon soy sauce
½ teaspoon turmeric
1 teaspoon freshly grated ginger
1 tablespoon fresh coriander
5 tablespoons peanut butter
½ cup water

Put all the ingredients except the water in a food processor or blender and process until blended thoroughly. Transfer the mixture to a bowl and slowly stir in the water. Mix until well blended. Serve at room temperature as a dip or as a sauce on cold beef.

(AMY SULLIVAN)

Dill Sauce
1 cup

½ pound sweet butter
½ cup chopped fresh dill
1 teaspoon chopped fresh rosemary
½ teaspoon nutmeg
2 teaspoons freshly squeezed lemon juice
Salt and freshly ground black pepper to taste

Melt the butter in the top of a double boiler. Add the dill, rosemary and nutmeg. Gently simmer for 5 minutes, stirring occasionally. Add the lemon juice and mix well. Season with salt and pepper. Serve over cooked vegetables or fish.

(ROBERT CHAPMAN)

Ginger Marinade
1 cup

½ cup soy sauce
2 tablespoons freshly grated ginger
½ cup dry or cream sherry
2 tablespoons honey
2 cloves garlic, crushed

Combine all the ingredients.
    A 2- to 3-pound steak marinated in this for at least an hour, preferably 2 hours, at room temperature will take less time to cook than if it were not marinated.

(GENE BOUCHER)

Mint Sauce
About 1 cup

1 cup mint leaves, stems and all
Juice of 3 lemons
½ cup olive oil
Salt and freshly ground black pepper to taste
2–3 cloves garlic

Combine all the ingredients in a blender and mix thoroughly. This sauce can be used as a marinade, or as a basting sauce during and after cooking. It can also be passed around at the table.

(B. KAY JONES CURLEY)

Water Mill Mint Vinegar
About 1 quart

2 cups fresh young spearmint leaves, finely chopped
1 cup sugar
1 quart cider vinegar

Combine the spearmint leaves and sugar, and let stand for 5 minutes.

Boil the vinegar for 1 minute. Add the spearmint leaves and sugar, crushing the leaves into the vinegar. Simmer for 3 minutes. Strain through cheesecloth and pour into hot sterilized jars. Cap tightly and let "ripen" for at least 3 weeks.

(MRS. SAMUEL SWINT)

Maryland Crab Cakes

8 patties

1 tablespoon butter
1 teaspoon flour
¼ cup heavy cream
½ pound crab meat, well picked over
1 tablespoon minced green peppers
¼ cup bread crumbs
Salt and freshly ground black pepper to taste
1 small onion, finely chopped
1 hard-cooked egg, finely chopped
1 egg, beaten
1 teaspoon dry mustard
½ teaspoon minced fresh tarragon
¼ teaspoon minced fresh rosemary
¼ teaspoon minced fresh oregano
Dash of paprika and cayenne pepper
½ teaspoon Worcestershire sauce, optional

Melt the butter in a heavy skillet over low heat. Add the flour, stirring well. Gradually add the cream and cook for 5 minutes, stirring frequently. Remove from the heat, add the remaining ingredients and let stand for 15 minutes. Form 8 patties and brown in butter in a heavy skillet.

(C. B. PECK)

Sorrel Soup

8–10 servings

1 pound sorrel, washed and stems removed
4 tablespoons butter
4 potatoes, peeled and diced
2½ quarts chicken broth
Salt, freshly ground black pepper and red pepper
  flakes to taste
1 cup heavy cream
Lemon slices for garnish

Chop the sorrel. Melt the butter in a saucepan. Add the sorrel and cook until the leaves are wilted. Stir in the potatoes and chicken broth. Cook, uncovered, for about 45 minutes, or until the potatoes are soft.

Pour the soup into a blender or food processor and process until smooth. Chill. Add seasonings and cream. Spoon into individual soup bowls and garnish each bowl with a lemon slice.

(NORA EPHRON)

Green Risotto with Sorrel
6 servings

2 tablespoons olive oil
6 tablespoons butter
½ cup finely chopped carrot (about 1 large carrot)
1 cup finely chopped onion (about 1 medium onion)
1 cup finely chopped fennel or celery (about 2 small
  fennel bulbs, trimmed, or 2 stalks celery)
4 cups tightly packed chopped sorrel (about 1 pound)
2 cups rice (preferably Italian short-grain arborio *rice)*
Salt and freshly ground black pepper to taste
4 cups chicken broth
1½ cups freshly grated imported Parmesan cheese

Melt the oil and 4 tablespoons of the butter in a heavy skillet over low heat. Add the carrot, onion and fennel to the skillet and cook for 10 minutes, stirring constantly to prevent sticking. (All the vegetables can be chopped in a food processor by turning the motor on and off quickly for a few seconds; do not overprocess. Discard the stems of the sorrel before you chop the sorrel leaves.)

Add all but 1 cup of the chopped sorrel and cook, stirring, for 2 minutes more. Add the rice and stir until completely coated with the vegetable mixture. Season with salt and pepper.

Add 3 cups of the chicken broth and bring to a boil, stirring occasionally. As the broth cooks away, gradually add the remaining broth to keep the rice just covered. Simmer, uncovered, for about 15 minutes, or until the rice is barely tender.

About 2 minutes before you expect it to be ready, stir in the remaining cup of chopped sorrel.

Remove from the heat and stir in the remaining butter and ½ cup of the Parmesan cheese. Let the risotto stand for 2–3 minutes before serving. Correct the seasonings. Pass the remaining cheese separately.

(ROBERT FIZDALE AND ARTHUR GOLD)

Sorrel Mayonnaise
2 cups

4 cups fresh sorrel leaves
3 tablespoons fresh Italian parsley
1 large cornichon (or 1 gherkin)
1 large egg
2 tablespoons freshly squeezed lemon juice
1 teaspoon imported prepared mustard, such as Dijon
1 teaspoon ground nutmeg
1½ cups safflower oil
Salt and freshly ground white pepper to taste

Dip the sorrel leaves into boiling water to eliminate the bitter taste. Drain and pat dry.

In a blender or food processor, combine the sorrel, parsley and *cornichon,* and process for about 2 seconds with the metal blade to mince.

Add the egg, lemon juice, mustard, nutmeg and 2 tablespoons of the oil. Process until the mixture thickens, about 8 seconds.

With the machine running, drizzle oil through the feed tube, allowing the mayonnaise to thicken as the oil is slowly added. Once the mayonnaise has thickened, the oil can be added more quickly. Add salt and pepper.

Sorrel Mayonnaise is excellent on cold poached fish with a garnish of capers.

(THE PORTABLE EPICURE, LTD.)

Patty's Pasta

2 servings

24 squares of fresh spinach or cheese ravioli
3 tablespoons butter
1 scallion, chopped (green and white portions)
½ teaspoon chopped fresh thyme
½ teaspoon chopped fresh parsley
2 tablespoons pignoli nuts
2 tablespoons fresh or dried funghi porcini
1 cup crème fraîche *(recipe follows)*
½ cup freshly grated Parmesan cheese
Salt and freshly ground black pepper to taste

Cook the ravioli in boiling salted water for 7 minutes. Drain and set aside.

Melt 2 tablespoons of the butter in a skillet over low heat. Sauté the scallion, thyme, parsley, pignoli nuts and *porcini* for 3–4 minutes. Set aside.

Put the remaining butter in a bowl and stir in the *crème fraîche* and cheese. Add the still warm ravioli and the sautéed mixture immediately. Season to taste with salt and pepper. Toss and serve.

("I invented this coming home to Manhattan after the Green Thumb 'pit stop.' It is rich and filling, and yummy." —PATRICIA ZOHN)

BASIC CRÈME FRAÎCHE

1 cup

1 teaspoon buttermilk
1 cup heavy cream

Add the buttermilk to the heavy cream and place the mixture in a jar and shake it. Let the mixture stand at room temperature, uncovered, for one or more days, until it thickens. Then cover and refrigerate; it will keep for several weeks. Ultrapasteurized cream takes longer to thicken than regular old-fashioned cream.

Baked Lemon Chicken with Thyme
2–4 servings

1 3-pound chicken, cut into serving pieces
4 cloves garlic, minced
4½ tablespoons butter
Salt and freshly ground black pepper to taste
2 large onions, sliced
Juice of 4 lemons
½ cup fresh thyme, leaves only
Sliced lemons

Preheat the oven to 350°.

Place the chicken in a baking dish. Rub the chicken with the garlic. Dot with the butter, sprinkle with salt and pepper, and place the sliced onions on top. Pour lemon juice over the chicken, then smother with the fresh thyme.

Bake for about 1 hour and 15 minutes, or until tender. Baste every 15 minutes. Serve with sliced lemons on top.

(MARY FORRISTAL)

Watercress Soup

About 2 quarts

2 pounds potatoes, boiled and peeled
8 scallions, chopped (green and white parts)
5 cups chicken broth
1½ bunches fresh watercress
2 teaspoons chopped fresh dill
1 teaspoon fresh marjoram
Salt to taste
1 egg
6 ounces cream cheese
1 cup heavy cream

Combine all the ingredients in a blender or food processor and process until smooth. May be served chilled or at room temperature.

(C. B. PECK)

Watercress and Leek Soup
6–8 servings

4 tablespoons butter
1½ cups minced leeks
1 cup minced onions
1 garlic clove, minced
2 potatoes, peeled and thinly sliced
2 bunches fresh watercress, coarsely chopped
4 cups chicken broth
1 cup milk
1 cup light cream
Salt and freshly ground black pepper to taste
Watercress leaves for garnish

Place the first 4 ingredients in a heavy saucepan and cook over low heat, stirring occasionally, for about 20 minutes, or until the vegetables are tender.

Add the potatoes, watercress and chicken broth. Simmer for another 25 minutes.

Pour the soup into a blender or food processor and process until smooth. Return the soup to the saucepan, stir in the milk and cream, and season with salt and pepper. Ladle into soup bowls and garnish with watercress leaves.

(CHARLES MANN)

HORSERADISH

Apple Horseradish Sauce
Approximately 1 cup

¼ cup freshly grated horseradish
1 cup homemade applesauce
1 teaspoon lemon juice
Salt to taste

Combine all the ingredients and chill. Serve as an accompaniment to pork roast.

(BETTY PELL)

Horseradish Sauce for Beef
Approximately ¾ cup

3 tablespoons freshly grated horseradish
1½ tablespoons mild white vinegar or lemon juice
½ teaspoon sugar
½ teaspoon salt
6 tablespoons heavy cream

Combine all the ingredients except the cream. Whip the cream until stiff, and beat it into the mixture. Chill.

(BETTY PELL)

Horseradish Dip for Raw Vegetables
About 1 pint

3 tablespoons freshly grated horseradish
1 cup mayonnaise
¼ cup heavy cream
½ cup ketchup
2 teaspoons tarragon vinegar
1 teaspoon freshly squeezed lemon juice
Salt and freshly ground black pepper to taste

Combine all the ingredients in a bowl and blend thoroughly. Chill. Suggested raw vegetables: turnip, fennel, cauliflower, cucumber, assorted peppers. Garnish with cherry tomatoes and black olives.

(BETTY PELL)

MUSHROOMS

Harry's Mushrooms

Large fresh mushroom caps, wild if possible
Salt

Do not wash the mushrooms. If dirty, wipe with a clean, damp cloth. Remove the stems. Fill each mushroom cap with a pinch of salt and place directly on top of a wood stove, iron stove, griddle or iron skillet over low heat. Watch them carefully.

The caps will warm, and the salt will draw out the water to make a teaspoon or less of mushroom liquor in the bottom of the cup-shaped cap.

Pass and serve with cocktails. The lucky eater first drinks the warm juice, then swallows its container.

("I learned this recipe from H. A. L. (Harry) Craig, the late Irish writer, who often made his mushrooms here on Long Island using domestic mushrooms. He always said The Green Thumb vegetables were as fresh as those of his native Limerick, and they have been much enjoyed here in Wainscott."—SHANA ALEXANDER)

Ham-Filled Mushrooms

1 pound mushrooms (caps should be the size of
  half-dollars)
¼ cup oil
1 small onion, finely chopped
1 clove garlic, minced
¼ cup finely chopped ham
½ cup Italian bread crumbs
2 tablespoons freshly grated Parmesan cheese
1 tablespoon minced fresh parsley
Fresh oregano to taste
Salt and freshly ground black pepper to taste
1 egg, beaten

Preheat the oven to 325°.

Clean the mushrooms. Remove the stems and spoon out a little of the inside cap. Finely chop enough stems to make ½ cup.

Heat the oil in a heavy skillet over low heat. Add the caps and toss to coat with the oil, then remove from the skillet.

Add the mushroom stems, onion and garlic to the skillet and

sauté until the onion is soft. Remove the pan from the heat and stir in the ham, bread crumbs, cheese, parsley, oregano, salt, pepper and egg.

When thoroughly blended, spoon the mixture into the mushroom caps. Arrange the caps on a baking sheet and drizzle a little oil over them. Bake for 15–20 minutes.

(MARIE WELLEN)

Stuffed Mushrooms

*½ pound large fresh mushrooms, cleaned
  but not washed*
½ cup butter
½ cup minced onions
2 cloves garlic, crushed
3 tablespoons minced fresh parsley
¾ teaspoon salt
½ teaspoon minced fresh oregano
½ cup seasoned bread crumbs
¼ cup freshly grated imported Parmesan cheese
Dash of red or white wine

Remove and finely chop the mushroom stems. Place the mushroom caps in a baking pan or on a cookie sheet and set aside.

Melt the butter in a heavy skillet over low heat. Add the chopped stems, onions, garlic, parsley, salt and oregano. Sauté until the onions are soft and transparent. Stir in the bread crumbs, cheese and wine. Blend well and remove from the heat.

Stuff the mushroom caps with the mixture. Broil for 8 minutes, or until the mushrooms are brown and tender.

(LINDA McLANE EUELL)

Upside-Down Mushrooms in Mustard Sauce

6 servings

2 tablespoons finely chopped shallots
½ cup dry white wine
¾ cup heavy cream
*2 heaping tablespoons imported prepared mustard, such
  as Dijon*
Salt and freshly ground black pepper to taste
*1 pound large fresh mushrooms, cleaned but not washed,
  stems removed*
Fresh parsley and julienne-cut carrots for garnish

Combine the shallots and wine in a heavy skillet. Cook over medium-high heat until the liquid is reduced to about ¼ cup. Lower the heat and add the cream, mustard, salt and pepper. Continue cooking, stirring occasionally, for another 3–4 minutes over medium heat.

Place the mushrooms upside down, resting on their caps, in the sauce. Lower the heat and cook for 5 more minutes. Do not stir. Mushrooms will open up and flatten out completely, looking like exotic flowers.

Carefully transfer to a platter. Garnish with fresh parsley and julienne-cut carrots.

(SUSAN BEITCHMAN)

Creamed Mushrooms and Eggs

2–4 servings

3 tablespoons butter
½ pound mushrooms, wiped with a damp cloth
  but not washed, sliced
2 tablespoons flour
1¼ cups milk
Salt and freshly ground black pepper to taste
3 hard-cooked eggs, sliced
Dash of Worcestershire sauce, optional
2–4 pieces of toast

Melt the butter in a heavy skillet over low heat. Add the mushrooms and sauté 7–10 minutes. Sprinkle the flour over the mushrooms (they will be juicy). Stir in the milk slowly, and add salt and pepper. Stir constantly and gently; the sauce will thicken.

Add the eggs and Worcestershire sauce, and stir until well blended. Remove from the heat and serve immediately on toast.

("An old family recipe . . ."—MRS. PAUL NUGENT)

Filets of Flounder Bonne Femme

4 servings

8 tablespoons butter
4 shallots, finely chopped
½ pound fresh mushrooms, with stems
8 flounder filets
2 tablespoons minced fresh parsley
1½ cups dry white wine
Salt and freshly ground white pepper to taste
2 teaspoons freshly squeezed lemon juice
6 sprigs parsley for garnish

Melt the butter in a large skillet over low heat. Add the shallots, half the mushrooms and the fish. Cover with the remaining mushrooms and the parsley. Pour in the wine and sprinkle with salt and pepper. Raise the heat to almost boiling and cook for 8 minutes.

Transfer the fish to a warm serving platter. Add the lemon juice to the skillet and continue cooking for about 1 minute. Pour over the fish and garnish with parsley.

(DOOLITTLE'S RESTAURANT)

Georgica Scallops
4–6 servings

2 tablespoons butter
¼ cup white wine
Juice of ½ lemon
¾ pound fresh mushrooms, cleaned
  but not washed, sliced
2 tablespoons oil
2 cloves garlic, minced
Flour
1 pound fresh bay scallops
Salt to taste
1 large ripe tomato, finely chopped
2 tablespoons minced fresh parsley
½ cup light cream
Freshly ground black pepper to taste

Heat 1 tablespoon of the butter and the wine in a heavy sauce-pan over low heat. When the butter is melted, add the lemon juice and mushrooms, and cook for 5 minutes, stirring occasionally. Set aside.

Heat the oil and the remaining butter in a large heavy skillet; add the garlic and sauté.

Place the flour in a paper bag, add the scallops and shake to coat. Place the fish in the skillet and sauté together with the garlic until the scallops begin to show color, about 1–2 minutes. Sprinkle with salt.

Stir in the mushroom mixture and the tomato. Cook for 5 minutes or until the tomato is soft. Add the parsley and cream; this will thicken the sauce. Season with pepper. Serve on pasta or rice.

(**EUNICE JUCKETT**)

Lanza Pasta

6 servings

4 tablespoons butter
¼ cup olive oil
3 cloves garlic, minced
2 bunches scallions, chopped (green and white parts)
1 pound fresh mushrooms, cleaned but not washed, finely chopped
2 bunches parsley, finely chopped
2 7-ounce cans Italian tuna fish packed in oil
1½ pounds rotelle (spiral pasta)

Heat the butter and oil in a skillet over low heat. Add the garlic and scallions, and sauté until soft. Add the mushrooms and cook for 3–5 minutes. Add the parsley and the tuna with its oil. Simmer over low heat, stirring occasionally.

Cook the pasta until done and drain. Pour the hot vegetable-tuna mixture over the pasta and stir thoroughly. May be served hot or cold.

(BIANCA LANZA)

Fettuccine Golosa

4 servings

2 tablespoons olive oil
2 tablespoons butter
¾ cup sliced fresh mushrooms
1 clove garlic, crushed
½ pound prosciutto, cut into julienne strips
1 cup fresh tomatoes, peeled, seeded and chopped
½ teaspoon fresh sage
⅛ teaspoon grated nutmeg
½ cup heavy cream
Salt and freshly ground black pepper to taste
½ pound fresh fettuccine
½ cup freshly grated imported Parmesan cheese
¾ cup minced fresh parsley

Heat the oil and butter in a deep, heavy skillet over medium heat. Add the mushrooms and garlic, and sauté for 8–10 minutes, or until the mushrooms are golden brown. Add the prosciutto, tomatoes, sage, nutmeg, cream, salt and pepper. Stir constantly for about 4 minutes, or until the sauce has thickened slightly.

Meanwhile, cook the fettuccine until it is *al dente*. Put the drained fettuccine in a large heated bowl. Add half of the Parmesan cheese. Pour the sauce over the pasta and mix well. Stir in the parsley. Sprinkle the remaining cheese on top. Serve immediately. Best served with hot buttered Italian bread and thick tomato slices sprinkled with chopped basil.

(EDWIN COSSITT)

Coriander Mushrooms

4 servings

3 tablespoons butter
3 tablespoons olive oil
3 shallots, peeled and minced
1 clove garlic, peeled and minced
2 pounds fresh mushrooms, wiped clean and
* thickly sliced*
¼ cup chopped fresh coriander
Salt and freshly ground black pepper to taste

Melt the butter and oil in a heavy skillet over medium heat. Add the shallots and garlic, and sauté for 2 minutes.

Add the mushrooms and continue cooking until golden brown, about 7 minutes. Stir in the coriander and cook for 1 minute. Season with salt and pepper.

Mushroom Butter

1 pound butter
12 ounces fresh mushrooms, wiped clean
1 teaspoon cooking sherry
Salt, pepper and minced garlic to taste

Melt 2 tablespoons of the butter in a heavy skillet over medium heat, add the mushrooms and sauté until brown, about 5–7 minutes. Add 6 tablespoons of the butter and melt. Remove from the heat and process in a food processor or blender until smooth. Add the remaining butter and continue processing. Season with salt, pepper and garlic.

Allow the mixture to cool, and then process again until it

becomes homogenized. Refrigerate. Serve on crackers, raw vegetables, baked potatoes or steak.

(IRENE MULLER)

OKRA

Okra-Tomato Soup
4 servings

1 pound ripe tomatoes, peeled and coarsely chopped
1 cup water
1 pound fresh okra
3½–4 cups beef consommé
Salt and freshly ground black pepper to taste
3–4 teaspoons brown sugar
1 teaspoon Worcestershire sauce
1 cup hot boiled rice

Put the tomatoes and water in a heavy pot. Bring to a boil and add the okra. Simmer until the okra is tender.

Add the consommé, salt, pepper, sugar and Worcestershire sauce, and simmer for 10 minutes. Taste and correct seasonings. Serve hot, passing around the rice separately.

(AUGUSTA MAYNARD)

Okra Stew

4 servings

1 pound fresh okra
1 teaspoon salt
7 cups water
1 tablespoon olive oil
1 ounce salt pork
2 ounces cured ham, diced
1 onion, finely chopped
1 tomato, finely chopped
1 green pepper, finely chopped
2 sweet chili peppers, finely chopped
1 clove garlic, finely chopped
6 coriander leaves, finely chopped
¼ cup Fresh Tomato Sauce (see p. 180)
Salt to taste
½ pound potatoes, peeled and quartered

Cut off the ends of the okra and slice the pods in half. Combine the salt and 4 cups of the water, add the okra and soak for 1 hour.

Heat the olive oil in a large, heavy pot and rapidly brown the pork and ham in it. Lower the heat, add the onion, tomato, green pepper, chili peppers, garlic and coriander, and sauté for 10 minutes, stirring occasionally.

Drain the okra and rinse in clear water. Add to the pot, along with 3 cups of the water and the tomato sauce, salt and potatoes. Heat to a boil, reduce the heat to moderate, cover and cook for 30 minutes. Uncover and cook for another 20 minutes, or until the sauce thickens.

(NANCY WASSERMAN)

Shrimp-Okra Gumbo

8 servings

¼ cup all-purpose vegetable oil
¼ cup flour
7 tablespoons butter
2 large onions, chopped
4½ cups coarsely chopped fresh okra
2½ cups chopped seeded tomatoes
2 large green peppers, seeded and chopped
1 large red pepper, seeded and chopped
5 large garlic cloves, minced
2½ pounds fresh shrimp, shelled and deveined
2½ quarts boiling water
2 chicken bouillon cubes
Dried red pepper to taste
Salt to taste
3 bay leaves
2 teaspoons Worcestershire sauce
1 teaspoon ground allspice
½ teaspoon freshly ground black pepper
1 teaspoon minced fresh thyme leaves
5 cups hot cooked rice

Mix the oil and flour in a small saucepan. Cook over low heat, stirring frequently with a whisk until the roux is the color of dark mahogany, about 45 minutes. Set aside.

Melt 3 tablespoons of the butter in a large, heavy Dutch oven. Add the onions and sauté until soft, about 5 minutes. Stir in the okra. Sauté for 5 minutes and then add the tomatoes. Cook gently for 30 minutes, stirring frequently.

Melt the remaining butter in a large skillet, add the peppers and garlic, and sauté for 5 minutes. Add the shrimp and sauté until the shrimp turn pink, about 4 minutes. Add the shrimp mixture and all the remaining ingredients except the rice to the okra mixture. Stir in the reserved roux. Simmer, covered, for 1½ hours.

Remove from the heat and let stand for 10 minutes. Ladle into serving bowls, topping each bowl with a scoop of rice.

Farm-Style Okra

4 servings

¼ *cup olive oil*
2 cups finely chopped onions
2 tablespoons minced shallots
1 cup chopped celery
1 cup baby mushroom caps
2 cups diced sweet red peppers
2 cups thinly sliced okra
Salt and freshly ground black pepper to taste
1 cup water

Heat the oil in a frying pan, add the onions and shallots, and sauté until transparent. Add the celery and cook very gently for 5 minutes, then add the mushrooms, peppers and okra. Season with salt and pepper. Add the water, cover and simmer for 15–20 minutes, or until the okra is tender. Drain before serving in a heated dish.

Okra with Mustard Sauce

8 servings

3 pounds fresh young okra, trimmed
Dash of salt
4 egg yolks
3 tablespoons Dijon mustard
1½ tablespoons freshly squeezed lemon juice
3 small cloves garlic, minced
Salt and freshly ground black pepper to taste
1 cup cold sweet butter, cut into small pieces
2 tablespoons minced fresh thyme

Cook the okra with a dash of salt in boiling water to cover for 5 minutes. Drain and keep warm.

Combine the egg yolks, mustard, lemon juice, garlic, salt and pepper in a medium-sized saucepan. Cook over low heat, whisking in the butter, 1 piece at a time, until it is completely mixed and the sauce is thick (about 5 minutes). Stir in the thyme. Pour the sauce over the okra and serve immediately.

Okra with Warm Tomato Vinaigrette

6–8 servings

1 pound okra
4 tablespoons olive oil
4 tablespoons chopped shallots
1 cup chopped tomatoes
1 medium clove garlic, minced
4 tablespoons red wine vinegar
⅔ cup dry white wine
¼ teaspoon salt
Freshly ground black pepper to taste
2 tablespoons chopped gherkins
3 tablespoons small capers, drained

Cut off the stems and tips of the okra. Steam the okra for 5 minutes, until just tender. Set out to cool in a single layer. Do not refrigerate.

Heat the oil, add the shallots and sauté for a few minutes, until wilted. If using fresh tomatoes, dip into hot water for approximately 5 to 10 seconds, skin and squeeze out seeds and excess liquid. Measure and add to shallots. Cook over medium heat for 5 minutes. Add the garlic, vinegar, wine, salt and pepper. Cook for about 10 minutes to reduce to the consistency of ketchup. Stir in the gherkins and capers. Set aside.

Arrange the cooled okra on a platter and pour the sauce over it.

(LEE BAILEY)

ONIONS

French Onion Tart

16–18 servings as appetizer;
10–12 as dinner course

FILLING
5 tablespoons butter
3 pounds large onions, thinly sliced
½ tablespoon salt
¾ cup heavy cream
Freshly ground black pepper to taste

DOUGH
1 package active dry yeast
¾ cup tepid water
1½ tablespoons olive oil plus oil for brushing
2¼ cups unbleached flour
¾ teaspoon salt

1 cup finely grated Gruyère cheese
1 cup black olives, pitted and halved

Preheat the oven to 350°.

Melt the butter in a large, heavy skillet over low heat. Add the onions and salt, cover and cook over low heat for 1¼–1½ hours, stirring frequently. Do not let the onions brown or stick to the bottom of the pan.

Remove from the heat when the onions have turned a rich golden color and there is lots of juice in the skillet.

Strain the onions through a sieve over a bowl, pressing gently with a wooden spoon or spatula to squeeze out all the liquid. Set the onion pulp aside.

Combine the onion liquid and the heavy cream and cook until the liquid is reduced to ¾ cup. Mix with the onion pulp. Season with pepper and set aside.

To make the dough, dissolve the yeast in the water, then add the 1½ tablespoons of oil. Combine the flour and salt in a food processor fitted with a steel blade. With the food processor running, pour the yeast mixture through the feed tube. Run for 30 seconds, until the dough forms a ball.

Put the dough in a 2-quart bowl and let rise until doubled in size. Punch down. Roll out onto a lightly floured surface to fit a 17-inch round pan and transfer it to the pan. Brush with olive oil and let rise again.

Spread the onion-cream filling on the "pizza." Sprinkle with grated cheese and decorate with olives. Bake for 35–40 minutes.

(JANE COHLER ROSS)

Millet Burgers

4 servings

3 cups cooked millet
3 stalks celery, finely chopped
1 large onion, minced
3 eggs, beaten
½ cup bread crumbs
Oil for frying
Bread crumbs for coating

Combine the millet, celery and onion in a large mixing bowl. Slowly stir in the eggs and the ½ cup of bread crumbs. Mix well and let stand for 1 hour.

Heat some oil in a large, heavy skillet. Form the mixture into patties, coat with bread crumbs and fry until golden brown on both sides.

(DEBORAH PRICE)

Water Chestnut Relish

10 8-ounce jars

3 cups sugar
3 heaping tablespoons flour
1½ tablespoons dry mustard
1 tablespoon salt
¾ tablespoon turmeric
4 teaspoons celery seeds
3 cups cider vinegar
6 medium onions, finely chopped
2 green peppers, finely chopped
1 cucumber, peeled and diced
2 roasted pimientos, finely chopped
4 8½-ounce cans water chestnuts, chopped, not too fine

Mix the first 6 ingredients together and put in a saucepan with the vinegar. Bring to a steady boil. Add the onions, peppers, cucumber and pimientos, and boil for 3 minutes. Add the chestnuts and boil for 2 minutes.

Pour into hot sterilized jars and seal while the relish is still warm.

(HAMILTON DARBY)

P E P P E R S

Weakfish Salad

4 servings

2–3 cooked weakfish (poached or steamed), flaked
1 large red pepper, diced
½ cup finely chopped shallots
Zest of 1 lemon
½ cup finely chopped Italian parsley
¼ cup chopped capers
½ teaspoon celery seeds
1 tablespoon Dijon-style mustard
1 tablespoon tarragon vinegar
1 tablespoon freshly squeezed lemon juice
6–8 tablespoons olive oil
½ cup finely chopped fresh chives

Combine the first 7 ingredients. Make a vinaigrette dressing
using the remaining ingredients. Stir the dressing into the
weakfish salad and marinate at least ½ hour before serving.

(DANA JACOBI)

Rigatoni Neapolitan-Style with Sautéed Sweet Peppers

4–6 servings

3 fresh red peppers
3 fresh yellow peppers
4 tablespoons olive oil
4 whole garlic cloves, peeled
Salt to taste
1 pound rigatoni *(macaroni tubes)*
⅔ cup freshly grated Parmesan cheese
⅔ cup sliced black olives
¼ cup butter, melted
15–20 fresh basil leaves, chopped

Cut the peppers in half and discard the seeds. Remove the skin with a vegetable peeler and cut the peppers into ½-inch strips. Cut the strips in half. Set aside.

Heat 3 tablespoons of the oil in a heavy skillet over medium heat, add the garlic and sauté until light brown. Discard the garlic with a slotted spoon. Put the peppers in the skillet and cook over high heat for about 15 minutes, or until tender but not mushy. Remove from the skillet and salt lightly.

Boil 4–5 quarts of water with 1 tablespoon of oil. Add the pasta and cook until it is *al dente.* Drain and combine in a large warm bowl with the peppers, Parmesan cheese, olives, butter and basil leaves. Mix thoroughly before serving.

(MRS. PETER BOYLE)

Peppers à la Tobia

6 servings

12 peppers, red, yellow and green
12 cloves garlic, cut into thirds
¼ cup plus 2 tablespoons olive oil
3 medium-sized ripe tomatoes, chopped
¼ cup sweet vermouth
2 pinches dried red pepper
2 pinches freshly ground black pepper

Preheat the oven to 475°.

Cut the peppers in half and remove the seeds. Slice the peppers into ½-inch-wide strips. Place them in a roasting pan with the garlic and pour the ¼ cup of olive oil over them.

Heat the remaining olive oil in a heavy skillet, add the tomatoes and sauté for 5 minutes. Mix the tomatoes into the pepper mixture.

Add the vermouth, red pepper and black pepper, and blend thoroughly. Bake for 20–25 minutes, stirring occasionally. Remove from the oven and serve immediately.

(**STANLEY MOSS**)

Stuffed Peppers
4 servings

4 green peppers
½ cup cooked rice
1 pound chopped meat
2 eggs, beaten
¼ cup chopped fresh parsley
1 small onion, grated
Salt and freshly ground black pepper to taste
5–6 cups Fresh Tomato Sauce (see page 180)

Wash and core the peppers, being careful not to split them. Set aside.

Place the rice in a sieve and run hot water over it to remove the starch. Let it drip-dry. Set aside.

In a large mixing bowl, combine the meat, eggs, parsley, onion, salt and pepper. Blend thoroughly. Using your hands, mix in the rice until well blended.

Stuff the peppers with the mixture. Gently place them with the tomato sauce in a large pot. Bring to a boil, cover, reduce the heat and simmer for 1½ hours, turning the peppers sideways once or twice. Serve at once.

(JEAN GLASSELL)

Autumn Leaves

6 servings

2 large red peppers
2 large yellow peppers
1 large chocolate pepper
1 large green pepper
¼ cup olive oil
1 clove garlic, minced
1 tablespoon freshly squeezed lemon juice

Rinse and dry the peppers. Place them on a baking sheet and broil 4–5 inches from the heat for 7 minutes on each side, or until the entire surface is charred. Drop into a paper bag and seal. Allow to cool.

Peel off the pepper skins. Cut the peppers in half and remove the seeds. Then cut into strips and place in a bowl.

Combine the olive oil, garlic and lemon juice. Gently pour the dressing over the pepper strips and mix well. A colorful and delicious dish.

Pepper Relish

6 pints

12 green peppers
12 sweet red peppers
12 medium onions
1 pint vinegar
2 cups sugar
3 teaspoons salt

Finely chop the peppers and onions, draining off the juice. Add enough boiling water to cover and let stand for 5 minutes. Drain again.

Boil the vinegar, sugar and salt in a heavy saucepan. Add the drained peppers and onions, and continue boiling for 15 minutes longer. Pour into hot sterilized jars and cover.

(GRANNY HALSEY)

Hot Pepper Jelly
3 ½ cups

1½ cups finely chopped green peppers
½ cup finely chopped hot peppers
7½ cups sugar
1½ cups white vinegar
2 3-ounce packages of liquid fruit pectin
¼ teaspoon green food coloring, optional

Put the peppers in a food processor or blender and process until puréed. Combine the peppers, sugar and vinegar in a large stainless-steel saucepan and bring to a boil. Boil for 6 minutes, stirring constantly.

Add the pectin and continue to boil for another 3 minutes, stirring constantly. Stir in the food coloring.

Remove from the heat and skim off the foam. Quickly pour into hot sterilized jars, leaving ½-inch space on top. Cover at once with ⅛ inch of paraffin. Put on the lids.

Serve with a block of cream cheese and crackers as an hors d'oeuvre.

(SUSAN HALSEY)

NEW POTATOES

French Potato Salad
10 servings

3 pounds new potatoes
¼ cup wine vinegar
Salt and freshly ground black pepper to taste
3 tablespoons consommé
⅓ cup dry white wine
1 tablespoon fresh tarragon, chopped
½ teaspoon dry mustard
¼ cup chopped fresh dill
¼ cup chopped fresh parsley
1 tablespoon chopped fresh chives
¾ cup olive oil

Place the potatoes in a kettle and add enough cold water to cover. Bring to a boil and cook until tender, about 15 minutes. Remove from the heat and drain. Peel the potatoes and cut into ¼-inch-thick slices. Place in a large bowl and set aside.

Combine the remaining ingredients and mix well. Pour over the potatoes, tossing gently to coat thoroughly. Serve warm or let cool to room temperature. Before serving, toss again.

("The French in Tunisia, North Africa, where I come from, often enjoy potato salad like this with wine."—ANTOINETTE LASH)

New Potato and Bean Salad

8–10 servings

½ *pound sliced bacon, cut into 1-inch pieces*
3 *pounds small new red potatoes, washed, unpeeled and*
  cut into ¼-inch pieces
1 *pound fresh green beans, washed, trimmed and cut into*
  2-inch pieces
½ *cup salad oil*
¼ *cup tarragon vinegar*
¼ *cup beef consommé*
½ *cup chopped scallions (green and white parts)*
¼ *cup finely chopped fresh parsley*
1 *clove garlic, crushed*
Salt and freshly ground black pepper to taste
1 *teaspoon dry mustard*
1 *teaspoon minced fresh basil*

Cook the bacon until almost crisp. Drain on paper towels and set aside.

Put the potatoes in a kettle, add enough salted cold water to cover and bring to a boil. Cook until tender, about 10 minutes. Drain.

Steam the beans in a small amount of salted water until crisp-tender. Drain.

Combine the remaining ingredients and mix well. Set aside.

Put the warm potatoes and beans in a large bowl, pour the dressing over the vegetables and toss gently.

Add the drained bacon pieces and toss gently again. The potatoes will absorb most of the dressing mixture.

The salad can now be served, warm and delicious, or it can be covered and kept at room temperature for several hours.

(SYDNEY BALTERMAN)

Vichyssoise à la Ritz

8 servings

1¼ cups butter
4 leeks, trimmed, washed and sliced (white part only)
1 medium onion, sliced
5 medium potatoes, peeled and thinly sliced
1 quart chicken broth
Salt to taste
3 cups milk
2 cups heavy cream
Chopped chives for garnish

Melt the butter in a deep kettle over low heat, add the leeks and onion, and sauté until lightly browned. Add the potatoes, chicken broth and salt. Boil gently for 35 minutes, or until very tender.

Pour the mixture into a food processor or blender and process until smooth. Return the puréed mixture to the kettle. Stir in the milk and 1 cup of the cream and heat. Cool and purée again. Chill.

Stir in the remaining cream. Chill thoroughly and serve garnished with chives.

(MRS. HELEN MARINO)

Clam Chowder

4 servings

8 tablespoons butter
1 onion, chopped
3–4 cups clams with their juice
6–8 new potatoes, diced
2 carrots, peeled and diced
1 stalk celery, diced
1 quart half-and-half
Fresh chopped parsley for garnish
Salt and freshly ground black pepper to taste

Melt the butter in a large pot, add the onion and sauté.

Measure the clam juice and, if necessary, add water to make 2½ cups. Add the juice, potatoes, carrots and celery to the pot.

Chop the clams. Add them to the pot, cover and simmer, stirring occasionally, for at least 30 minutes.

Stir in the half-and-half and blend well. Ladle into warm soup bowls and garnish with fresh parsley. Pass the salt and pepper for individual seasoning.

(STACEY LAPUTZ)

Herbed New Potatoes
8 servings

3 pounds small new red potatoes
¼ cup dry vermouth
Salt and freshly ground black pepper to taste
4 tablespoons combined finely chopped fresh parsley, dill,
*   chives and basil*
½ cup imported olive oil

Boil the potatoes in their jackets for about 15 minutes, or until tender. When done, let dry on a cloth towel. Do not peel. Cut into eighths and place in a single layer in a casserole dish.

Heat the vermouth and pour over the potatoes. Sprinkle with salt, pepper and the fresh herbs. Turn the potatoes over and cover with a clean cloth. Do not refrigerate. Add the oil just before serving and mix.

(JEANNE WALLER)

RADISHES

Black Radish Vienna

1 black radish, 4 inches in diameter
Juice of ½ lemon
½ teaspoon salt
Pinch of freshly ground black pepper

Peel and coarsely grate the radish. Add the lemon juice, salt and pepper. Mix thoroughly.

Serve in a glass bowl with mugs of cold beer and some good black bread.

("My stepfather gave me this recipe. He knew it from his student days in Vienna, where he spent happy summer evenings eating pinches of radish and drinking beer in cafés with his friends. The idea, of course, is that the radish enhances one's appreciation of the beer, and vice versa!" —CAROL WILLIAMS)

SUMMER SQUASH

Zucchini Chips
About 7 dozen chips

3 medium zucchini, cut into ⅛-inch-thick slices
¾ cup bourbon
½ cup all-purpose flour
Salt and freshly ground black pepper to taste
½ cup butter or oil
Tarragon

Combine the zucchini and bourbon in a bowl and cover. Marinate in the refrigerator for 24 hours, turning several times.

Combine the flour, salt and pepper, and dredge the zucchini in the mixture. Fry in the butter until golden brown. Drain on paper towels. Sprinkle with tarragon before serving.

(CHARLOTTE SCHRAMM)

Zucchini French Fries

2 medium zucchini
Salt
¼ cup flour
Cooking oil

Peel the zucchini and cut crosswise or lengthwise into ½-inch squares about 2 inches long (just as you would cut potatoes for French fries). Sprinkle with salt and let drain for 45–60 minutes to get rid of excess moisture.

Pat dry and dredge with the flour in a paper bag. Shake off the excess flour and deep-fry in oil for about 2 minutes, or until golden brown. Drain on paper towels, sprinkle with salt and serve.

(JERRY MURPHY)

Zucchini Soup I
6–8 servings

5–6 medium zucchini
1 large onion, thinly sliced
1½ teaspoons curry powder
3 cups chicken broth
1 cup heavy cream
½ cup milk
Salt and freshly ground black pepper to taste

Cut all but one zucchini into 1-inch-thick slices, then quarter the slices. In a saucepan, combine the zucchini, onion, curry powder and chicken broth. Bring to a boil, cover and simmer for 45 minutes, or until the vegetables are tender.

Spoon the hot mixture into a food processor or blender and process until well puréed. Add the cream, milk, salt and pepper. Chill thoroughly.

Cut the remaining zucchini into matchstick-size pieces. Spoon the soup into chilled individual bowls and garnish each bowl with the zucchini pieces for added crunch!

(ANNA NOEL)

Zucchini Soup II
4–6 servings

4 cups chicken broth
1 medium onion, chopped
1 stalk celery, chopped
6 small zucchini, diced
6 sprigs fresh parsley
1 bay leaf
1 teaspoon fresh thyme
Salt and freshly ground black pepper to taste

In a large pot, combine all the ingredients. Bring to a boil, cover and simmer for about 30 minutes, or until the vegetables are tender.

Remove the bay leaf and pour the soup into a blender or food processor. Process until smooth. Serve hot or cold.

(CHI MARAN)

Zucchini Pancakes

3–4 servings

2 cups grated zucchini
2 eggs
¼ cup flour or wheat germ
½ teaspoon vanilla extract
¼ teaspoon freshly grated nutmeg
¼ teaspoon grated fresh ginger
Salt to taste
1–2 tablespoons safflower oil

Combine all the ingredients except the oil and stir until well blended.

Heat the oil in a heavy skillet over medium heat. Drop the batter by spoonfuls into the skillet and brown on each side. Serve hot as a vegetable side dish, or serve as a dessert, with honey or jam.

(**FLORENCE SCHUB**)

Zucchini Frittata

6–8 servings

3 cups grated zucchini
1 tablespoon salt
8 eggs, beaten
1 cup grated Swiss cheese
½ cup grated Parmesan cheese
¾ cup chopped green or sweet red peppers
½ cup chopped scallions (both green and white parts)
½ cup chopped fresh parsley
2 jalapeño peppers, finely chopped, optional
2 tablespoons butter

Preheat the oven to 400°.

Mix the zucchini with the salt and let stand for 15 minutes in a colander. Squeeze out as much of the liquid as possible.

In a large mixing bowl, combine the eggs, zucchini and all the remaining ingredients except the butter.

Heat the butter in a well-cured heavy skillet, and when bubbling, add the zucchini-egg mixture. Place at once in the oven and bake for 15 minutes, or until firm to the touch. Slice and serve from the pan.

("This recipe also makes an excellent hot appetizer if cooked in muffin tins, preferably Teflon-lined. Place about 1 heaping tablespoon of the mixture in each cup and bake for 10 minutes."—**BRENT NEWSOM, ANNEX RESTAURANT**)

Zucchini with Linguine

6 servings

3 tablespoons olive oil
1 large onion, chopped
2 cloves garlic, minced
2 large zucchini, thinly sliced
4 tomatoes, chopped
2 bay leaves
1 teaspoon fresh oregano
Handful chopped fresh parsley
1½ pounds linguine, cooked
Freshly grated imported Parmesan cheese

Heat the oil in a large skillet, add the onion and garlic, and sauté over medium heat until golden brown. Remove the onion and garlic with a slotted spoon and set aside.

Add the zucchini and tomatoes to the skillet and cook until almost soft. Stir in the onion, garlic and herbs. Cook slowly over low heat for about 30 minutes, stirring often.

Combine the warm linguine and the zucchini mixture in a large bowl. Serve with grated Parmesan cheese.

(ANTOINETTE LASH)

Zucchini with Pasta
4–6 servings

2 tablespoons butter
2 tablespoons olive oil
5 small zucchini, cut into 1½-inch-long sticks
2 large onions, minced
1 clove garlic, minced
1 cup heavy cream
1 pound cooked farfel
1½ cups freshly grated Parmesan cheese
Salt and freshly ground black pepper to taste

Heat the butter and oil in a large skillet. Add the zucchini and sauté quickly. Remove the zucchini with a slotted spoon and set aside.

Add the onions to the skillet and sauté until soft and transparent. Add the garlic and cook another minute. Stir in the cream, bring to a boil and continue cooking until the sauce is reduced by one third.

Add the pasta, zucchini and ½ cup of the cheese. Stir thoroughly until well heated. Season with salt and pepper. Serve with the remaining cheese.

(JUDY LITTLE)

Lobster with Zucchini–Swiss Cheese Stuffing

4 servings

8 tablespoons butter
3 small zucchini, shredded
1 medium onion, finely chopped
2 large fresh mushrooms, finely chopped
1 clove garlic, minced
6 ounces Swiss Lorraine cheese, grated
½ cup bread crumbs
½ teaspoon minced fresh parsley
½ teaspoon minced fresh thyme
½ teaspoon poultry seasoning
Salt and freshly ground black pepper to taste
4 1½-pound lobsters
Lemon wedges

Preheat the oven to 450°.

Melt 2 tablespoons of the butter in a heavy skillet, add the zucchini, onion, mushrooms and garlic, and sauté until the onion is soft and transparent. In a medium-sized bowl, combine the cheese, bread crumbs and herbs with the sautéed vegetables. Add salt and pepper. Mix thoroughly and set aside.

Plunge the lobsters, head first, into 2 inches of boiling water and steam for 10 minutes. Remove them from the pot and place on a cutting board. When cool enough to handle, split the body section (not the tail) with a sharp knife and remove the green liver. Fill the cavity with the stuffing. Wrap each lobster with foil, exposing the stuffing area. Bake for 10 minutes, or until the stuffing is brown. Serve with lemon wedges and the remaining butter, which has been melted.

(KERRY MILLER)

Moroccan Vegetable Couscous

6 servings

1 pound couscous
2½ cups salted water
6 medium zucchini, sliced
2 large green peppers, sliced
2 large onions, quartered
3 medium potatoes, sliced
4 large carrots, quartered
1 small celery, sliced
7 cups cold water
3 ounces butter
1 pound dried or canned chick peas, cooked
⅓ cup blanched almonds
⅔ cup raisins
1 pound tomatoes, quartered
3 cloves garlic, crushed
1–3 green chili peppers, finely minced
2 teaspoons salt
1 teaspoon freshly ground black pepper
½ teaspoon red pepper
2 teaspoons ground cumin
2 teaspoons paprika
½ teaspoon ground saffron, dissolved in
  1 teaspoon hot water
3 teaspoons turmeric
2 teaspoons coriander
½ cup chopped fresh parsley
¼ teaspoon fresh ginger, minced
1 teaspoon tomato paste
Dash of cayenne pepper

Put the couscous into a large bowl with the salted water. Soak and then drain the excess liquid.

Combine the zucchini, peppers, onions, potatoes, carrots and celery in a large heavy pot. Add 5 cups of the cold water and bring to a boil. Reduce the heat and simmer for 30 minutes.

Add the butter, chick peas, almonds, raisins, tomatoes and the remaining 2 cups of water.

Stir in the garlic, chili peppers, salt, black and red pepper, cumin, paprika, saffron, turmeric, coriander and parsley. Bring to a boil, reduce the heat and simmer for 15 minutes. Stir in the couscous.

To make the sauce, strain off 1 cup of liquid from the vegetables and pour it into a small saucepan. Add the ginger, tomato paste and cayenne pepper, and bring to a boil.

Add to the vegetable mixture and mix well.

(GALE ALDRED)

Calabasas

4–6 servings

2 tablespoons butter
1 medium onion, chopped
2 medium zucchini, sliced
1 medium summer squash, sliced
2 ripe tomatoes, peeled and chopped coarsely
1 long hot pepper, seeded and finely minced
1 cup grated Monterey Jack or cheddar cheese
2 cloves garlic, minced
1 tablespoon minced fresh oregano
Salt and freshly ground black pepper to taste
2 heaping tablespoons fresh coriander

Preheat the oven to 350°.

Melt the butter in a heavy skillet over low heat, add the

onion and sauté until transparent. Stir in the zucchini and summer squash, and sauté slightly. Add all the remaining ingredients except the coriander and bake for 30–35 minutes. Sprinkle with coriander before serving.

(ELIZABETH CLARKE)

Mushroom- and Cheese-Stuffed Zucchini
10 servings

14 small zucchini
¼ cup olive oil, more if necessary
1½ cups finely diced onions
1½ cups chopped mushrooms
3 cloves garlic, minced
½ cup cream cheese
½ cup blue cheese
3 eggs, beaten
2 cups freshly grated Parmesan cheese
2 cups chopped fresh parsley
Salt and freshly ground black pepper to taste

Preheat the oven to 350°.

Blanch the zucchini in boiling salted water for 5 minutes. Drain well and trim the ends. Cut in half lengthwise. Remove the pulp and set aside. Reserve the zucchini shells.

Heat the oil in a heavy skillet, add the onions and sauté over medium heat until soft and transparent. Add the mushrooms and garlic, continuing to stir until the moisture from the mushrooms evaporates. Add the zucchini pulp and cook, stirring, until all the liquid evaporates. Remove from the heat.

Mix together the cream cheese, blue cheese, eggs, 1½ cups of the Parmesan cheese, and the parsley, salt and pepper.

Slowly add to the zucchini mixture, stirring constantly. Cook over low heat for 5 minutes.

Fill the zucchini shells with the mixture and top with the remaining Parmesan cheese. Bake for 10 minutes, then brown under the broiler.

(MELISSA LORD)

Zucchini Pesto
4–6 servings

6–8 medium zucchini, grated
1 tablespoon salt
2 cups fresh basil leaves
½ cup safflower oil
2 tablespoons pine nuts
2 cloves garlic, peeled and cut in quarters
½ teaspoon salt
½ cup 1-inch cubes of Parmesan cheese
3 tablespoons butter

Mix the zucchini with the salt and place in a colander for at least ½ hour to drain.

Meanwhile, put the basil leaves, oil, pine nuts, garlic, salt and cheese into a food processor. Process, scraping the sides occasionally, until well mixed.

Melt the butter in a heavy skillet and sauté the drained zucchini in it. When tender, transfer to a serving bowl and stir in the pesto.

(MARILYN HILLMAN)

Grilled Zucchini and Garlic

1 zucchini, thinly sliced
Minced garlic
Salt and freshly ground black pepper to taste
1 tablespoon imported olive oil

Tear off a large piece of aluminum foil and fold it double. Put the zucchini, garlic, salt and pepper in the center of the foil and drizzle the olive oil into the packet. Seal the packet tightly and cook on a grill for about 15 minutes.

(WENDY SAFFIR)

Zucchini Bread

2 loaves

3 eggs
2 cups sugar
1 cup oil
1 teaspoon salt
3 cups all-purpose flour
3 teaspoons ground cinnamon
¼ teaspoon baking powder
1 teaspoon baking soda
2 cups grated zucchini
3 teaspoons vanilla extract
1½ cups chopped walnuts or pecans
1 cup raisins, optional

Preheat the oven to 325°. Butter and flour 2 8½ × 4½ × 2½-inch loaf pans.

Beat the eggs in a large mixing bowl until foamy. Stir in the sugar and oil, and blend thoroughly.

Sift together the salt, flour, cinnamon, baking powder and baking soda. Add this to the egg mixture, a third at a time, beating thoroughly after each addition. The mixture should be stiff.

Add the zucchini and vanilla. Fold in the nuts and raisins. When thoroughly blended, pour the mixture into the prepared pans. Bake for 1 hour, or until a knife inserted into the center comes out clean.

(**MARGIE BURKE**)

Zucchini Cake with Cream Cheese Icing

12 servings

CAKE
4 eggs
1 cup sugar
1 cup vegetable oil
3 cups all-purpose flour
1 teaspoon salt
1½ teaspoons baking soda
2 teaspoons ground cinnamon
¾ teaspoon baking powder
2 cups grated zucchini
2 teaspoons vanilla extract
1 cup chopped walnuts

ICING
8 ounces cream cheese
½ cup sweet butter, softened
4 cups sifted powdered sugar

Preheat the oven to 350°. Grease and flour a 13 × 9 × 2-inch cake pan.

Beat the eggs with the sugar until fluffy. Add the oil and blend well.

Sift together the flour, salt, baking soda, cinnamon and baking powder. Add the zucchini alternately with the dry ingredients to the egg mixture. Blend well. Add the vanilla and blend again. Stir in the walnuts.

Pour the batter into the prepared cake pan and bake for 55 minutes, or until a knife inserted into the center comes out clean. Cool for 10 minutes, then remove from the pan to a wire rack. Cool completely before frosting.

To make the icing, mix together the cream cheese and butter until smooth. Stir in the powdered sugar slowly. Blend thoroughly.

(MARGARET ZORKO)

TOMATOES

Southern Italian Tomato Salad

2–3 servings

1 clove garlic, peeled and halved
3–4 firm ripe tomatoes
1 tablespoon wine vinegar
½ teaspoon fresh oregano
10–15 large fresh basil leaves, torn
Freshly ground black pepper to taste
Coarse salt to taste

Place the garlic halves in a bowl. Cut the tomatoes in eighths lengthwise and then in half crosswise to make chunks, and add to the bowl. Sprinkle with the vinegar.

Add the oregano, basil leaves and a grinding of pepper. Mix well and let stand at room temperature for at least ½ hour. Sprinkle with salt and mix lightly just before serving, at which time the garlic halves can be removed.

("In the artists' *trattoria* on Via della Croce in Rome, tomatoes are served with basil and oil only, while the southern Italians—Calabrians and Sicilians—add oregano and garlic."—**ELIZABETH FISHER**)

Middle East Tabouleh Salad

8 servings

1 cup bulghur wheat
2½ cups cold water
3–4 ripe tomatoes, diced
1 cup chopped fresh parsley
½ cup chopped scallions (green and white parts)
4 tablespoons olive or salad oil
4 tablespoons lemon juice or your favorite vinegar
Romaine lettuce leaves

Place the bulghur wheat and water in a large bowl and let stand for 1½ hours. Drain the bulghur well, pressing out any excess water after draining. This is done by covering the bulghur with waxed paper, turning the bowl on its side and pressing out the water with the palm of the hand.

Add the remaining ingredients and refrigerate for at least 1 hour to blend the flavors.

To eat Middle East style, serve on a bed of romaine lettuce leaves and use the leaves to pick up the salad and eat it with your fingers; or wrap the salad in individual romaine leaves, arrange on a platter and eat it with your fingers.

For variety, use chopped celery, black olives, or green or sweet red peppers.

(BARBARA ACTON)

Grandmother's Chili Sauce
12 cups

4 large onions
4 large green peppers
2 dozen large ripe tomatoes
5 cups vinegar
8 tablespoons sugar
2 tablespoons salt
1 tablespoon ground cinnamon
1 tablespoon ground cloves
1 tablespoon allspice
Pinch of cayenne pepper

Put the onions and peppers through a grinder separately. Chop the tomatoes and boil for 1 minute. Drain off most of the water and foam. Add the remaining ingredients and keep at a slow boil for 1½ hours. The fragrance is tantalizing!
    Put into sterilized jars and seal.

("My grandmother learned this as a new bride when she came to Long Island from Scotland, and passed it on to my mother, who, in turn, passed it on to me."—EUNICE JUCKETT)

Tomato and Dill Soup

4 servings

2 tablespoons butter
1 large onion, chopped
3 cloves garlic, minced
½ bunch scallions, chopped
6 large ripe tomatoes, peeled, seeded and quartered
Salt and freshly ground black pepper to taste
3 tablespoons tomato paste
4 tablespoons all-purpose flour
3–4 cups chicken broth or water
½ cup minced fresh dill

Melt the butter in a large saucepan over low heat. Add the onion and garlic, and sauté until the onion is soft and transparent.

Add the scallions, tomatoes, salt and pepper. Cook, uncovered, over medium heat for 10–15 minutes, stirring occasionally.

Stir in the tomato paste and flour. Add the chicken broth. Bring to a boil, lower the heat, add the dill and simmer for 15 minutes. Remove from the heat.

Cool to room temperature. Pour the soup into a food processor or blender and process until smooth. May be served piping hot or chilled.

(STANLEY AIGES)

Dad's Gazpacho

6 servings

4 ripe tomatoes, peeled and quartered
½ green pepper, seeded and sliced
½ onion, sliced
1 cucumber, peeled and sliced
Generous sprigs of fresh basil and parsley
1 clove garlic
Few drops of Tabasco
1 teaspoon salt
¼ teaspoon freshly ground black pepper
2 tablespoons olive oil
3 tablespoons wine vinegar
½ cup ice water
Croutons

Put all the ingredients except the croutons in a blender or food processor (two loads may be necessary). Cover and process for 4–5 seconds, until the vegetables are coarsely chopped. Chill. Serve with an ice cube and some croutons in each soup bowl.

(GLYNN MAPES)

Pasta alla Cecca

4 Servings

5 large tomatoes
4 cups chopped fresh basil
½ cup olive oil
Salt and red pepper flakes to taste
Pinch of sugar
1 clove garlic, halved
1 pound vermicelli or linguine

Plunge the tomatoes in boiling water for 1 full minute. Peel, seed and chop. In a large bowl, combine the tomatoes, basil, oil, salt, pepper, sugar and garlic. Let stand for at least 1 hour.

Boil the pasta until it is *al dente.* Remove the garlic halves from the sauce and discard. While the pasta is still warm, add the sauce and mix well. Serve immediately.

(NORA EPHRON)

Flounder Filet Eva

4 servings

2 pounds flounder filets
Salt and pepper to taste
4 tablespoons butter
3 medium onions, finely chopped
4–6 tomatoes, peeled, seeded and quartered

Preheat the oven to 375°.

Lightly season the filets with salt and pepper, fold in half and arrange in a buttered baking dish so that each filet slightly overlaps the next one.

Melt the butter in a heavy skillet over low heat, add the onions and sauté until soft but not brown. Add the tomatoes and simmer, uncovered, until the vegetables make a thick sauce. Season with additional salt and pepper, and spread the sauce over the fish.

Cover with waxed paper and bake for 17 minutes. Serve immediately.

(ANN SOBOTKA)

Bouillabaisse
8–10 servings

½ cup dark olive oil
2 large leeks, sliced (white part only)
1½ cups coarsely chopped onions
½ cup chopped green peppers
½ cup chopped red peppers
3 garlic cloves, crushed
4 teaspoons chopped fresh thyme
2 cups chopped fresh parsley
6 teaspoons chopped fresh basil
3 pounds ripe tomatoes, chopped
1 cup tomato purée
4 cups fish stock (recipe follows)
2 cups dry white wine
3 bay leaves
2 pounds firm-fleshed white fish, cut into bite-size pieces
20 raw shrimp, shelled and deveined
20 well-washed cherrystone clams
1½ quarts fresh mussels, cleaned and debearded
1 1½-pound lobster tail
Salt and freshly ground black pepper to taste

Heat the oil in a large pot. Add the leeks, onions and peppers, and cook over medium heat, stirring frequently, until the vegetables wilt.

Add the garlic, thyme, parsley and basil, and continue cooking, stirring constantly.

Add the tomatoes and tomato purée, and continue stirring for 1 minute. Blend in the fish stock and wine, and simmer for 30 minutes.

Put ⅓ of the mixture in a food processor and purée. Return the puréed mixture to the soup pot. Add the bay leaves. Bring to a boil and add the fish. Cook for about 5 minutes and add the shrimp. Simmer for about 8 minutes and add the clams, mussels and lobster tail. Cook, stirring gently, for about 5 minutes, or until the clams and mussels open. Season with salt and pepper. Serve in very hot bowls.

FISH STOCK

2 quarts cold water
1½ pounds non-oily fish spines and heads
2 bay leaves
1 carrot, chopped
1 celery rib, split
8 peppercorns
6 parsley sprigs

Combine all the ingredients in a large pot and simmer for 20 minutes. Strain and use broth for soups.

(ASHLEY DUBOIS)

Towd Point Mussels
4–6 servings

4 quarts fresh mussels
2 tablespoons olive oil
1 large onion, chopped
2 cloves garlic, minced
3 cups diced fresh ripe tomatoes
30 fresh basil leaves, chopped
5 fresh oregano sprigs, chopped
1 bottle good beer

Wash and debeard the mussels. Set aside.

Heat the oil in a large pot, add the onion and sauté until transparent. Add the garlic and continue sautéing. Stir in the tomatoes and herbs. Cook together for 1–2 minutes over high heat.

Add the beer and the mussels. Cover and cook over medium heat until the mussels open, about 5 minutes.

Serve the mussels and broth in large soup bowls. Have lots of good bread for dunking!

(ELLEN ZIMMERMAN)

Scallops Provençale
with Pasta

4 servings

3 tablespoons light olive oil
3 tablespoons butter
1 pound fresh bay scallops
8 shallots, minced
1 bunch scallions, chopped (both green and white parts)
3 large cloves garlic, minced
2½ tablespoons minced fresh basil
2 tablespoons minced fresh tarragon
½ cup dry white wine
12 medium tomatoes, peeled, seeded and chopped
½ cup heavy cream
1 teaspoon sugar
Salt and freshly ground black pepper to taste
1 pound linguine, freshly cooked
1 large ripe avocado, peeled, pitted and chopped

Heat the oil and butter in a large skillet over medium heat. Add the scallops and sauté until barely firm, about 2 minutes. Using a slotted spoon, transfer the scallops to a mixing bowl.

Sauté the shallots and scallions until soft. Stir in the garlic and herbs, and cook for 1 minute. Add the wine and cook for 2 minutes more. Stir in the tomatoes. Increase the heat to high and boil until the sauce is thick.

Stir in the cream and sugar and cook for another 20 seconds. Season with salt and pepper.

Pour over the scallops and mix gently. Add the hot pasta and toss lightly. Place on individual serving plates and top with the avocado.

Salsa Fresca

1 quart

2 white onions, finely chopped
2 large tomatoes, finely chopped
3 cloves garlic, minced
5 hot peppers or, if available, jalapeño peppers (seed if
  using jalapeño peppers or if milder sauce is desired)
Freshly chopped coriander
Touch of oregano
Salt to taste
Olive oil for sautéing

Combine all the ingredients and sauté in the olive oil until soft.
Use as a garnish for any Mexican dish.

(BETTY CLARK)

Tomato Sauce with Rosemary and Pancetta

6–8 servings

2 pounds fresh ripe tomatoes
⅔ cup chopped carrots
⅔ cup chopped celery
⅔ cup chopped onions
3 cloves garlic, chopped
Salt to taste
¼ teaspoon granulated sugar
½ cup imported olive oil
2 teaspoons finely chopped fresh rosemary leaves
½ cup thin strips of rolled pancetta *or prosciutto*

Wash the tomatoes in cold water and cut in half. Place in a saucepan and cook, covered, over medium heat for 10 minutes. Add the carrots, celery, onions, garlic, salt and sugar. Cook at a steady simmer, uncovered, for 30 minutes. Pour the mixture into a blender or food processor and process until smooth. Set aside.

Heat the oil in a small skillet over medium heat. When hot, add the rosemary and *pancetta* strips. Sauté for 1 minute, stirring constantly.

Combine the oil mixture with the tomato sauce in a saucepan and cook at a steady simmer, uncovered, for 15 minutes. Taste and correct the salt.

This savory sauce is particularly good with ziti or *penne rigati.* It has a delicate fresh flavor—the sweet taste is wonderful for a summer supper.

(SAN GIOVANNI FOOD STORE, SOUTHAMPTON)

Fresh Tomato Sauce

1 ½ cups

¼ cup imported olive oil
2 cloves garlic, split
1½ pounds fresh tomatoes, peeled and diced
1½ teaspoons salt
½ teaspoon freshly ground black pepper
3 tablespoons minced fresh Italian parsley

Heat the oil in a heavy saucepan. Brown the garlic in it and discard. Add the tomatoes, salt and pepper to the oil. Cook over low heat for 20 minutes, or until most of the water evaporates. Remove from the heat and gently stir in the parsley.

(PEARL BORGIA)

Tomato-Spice Cake

12 servings

6 medium tomatoes, peeled and seeded
4 cups all-purpose flour
2½ cups sugar
½ cup sweet butter
2½ teaspoons baking soda
2½ teaspoons ground cinnamon
2 teaspoons vanilla extract
1½ teaspoons salt
1 teaspoon nutmeg
1 teaspoon ground cloves
½ cup chopped walnuts

Preheat the oven to 350°. Grease a 10-inch tube pan.

Place the tomatoes in a blender or food processor and process until smooth. In a large bowl, combine the tomatoes (there should be 2½ cups of puréed tomatoes) with all the remaining ingredients except the walnuts. Mix until smooth.

Pour the batter into the prepared pan and sprinkle the top with the walnuts. Bake for 65–70 minutes, or until a knife inserted into the center comes out clean. Cool in the pan for 10 minutes. Remove and serve.

(SUSAN COLLEDGE)

Fulling Mill Farm
Green Tomato Relish

6 quarts

24 medium-sized green tomatoes, thinly sliced
6 green peppers, diced
12 medium onions, thinly sliced
2½ tablespoons salt
3 quarts white vinegar
4 cups sugar
1 tablespoon allspice
1 tablespoon ground cinnamon
1 tablespoon ground cloves
1 tablespoon mustard seed, **optional**

Sprinkle the tomatoes, peppers and onions with the salt and let stand, covered, overnight. Drain.

Place all the ingredients in a large, heavy cooking pot and simmer for 1 hour and 15 minutes, stirring occasionally. Place in hot sterilized jars and cap; it is not necessary to seal the jars.

(**EUNICE JUCKETT**)

Dolores's Piccalilli

12 pints

12 pounds green tomatoes, washed and coarsely chopped
5 pounds sweet red peppers, washed, seeded and coarsely
  chopped
5 pounds sweet green peppers, washed, seeded and
  coarsely chopped
1½ pounds onions, peeled and quartered
3 quarts cider vinegar
7 cups sugar
½ cup salt
1 cup mustard seed
3 tablespoons celery seed
1 tablespoon ground cinnamon
1 tablespoon allspice

Place the tomatoes, peppers and onions in a colander and drain. Discard the liquid.

Place the vegetables in a large, heavy pot and add 2 quarts of the vinegar. Boil, uncovered, for 30 minutes, stirring frequently. Drain the vegetables and discard the liquid.

Return the drained vegetables to the pot. Add the remaining vinegar and the sugar, salt, mustard seed, celery seed, cinnamon and allspice. Simmer, uncovered, for 3 minutes, stirring occasionally.

Pour immediately into clean hot sterilized jars, leaving a 1-inch space at the top. Pour in ½ inch of melted paraffin to seal.

(DOLORES NEEDHAM)

AUTUMN

Golden Beet Salad

6 servings

2 bunches golden beets, trimmed but not peeled
4 tablespoons mayonnaise
1 tablespoon imported prepared mustard, such as Dijon
1 bunch fresh dill

Put the beets in a saucepan of cold water to cover, bring to a boil, reduce the heat and simmer until tender, about 15–30 minutes, depending on the size of the beets. Let them cool in the cooking liquid, then remove and slip off the skins under cold running water. Cut the beets into julienne strips and set aside.

Mix the mayonnaise and mustard together. Chop ¼ cup of the dill and add to the mixture. Blend the mixture with the beets. Serve in glass bowls garnished with the remaining dill.

(**STEVEN PHILIPS**)

Borscht

6 servings

1 pound lean beef, cut into cubes
1½ quarts water
1 tablespoon salt
Freshly ground black pepper to taste
¼ cup shredded raw beets
1½ cups shredded raw carrots
2 tablespoons butter
1 medium onion, chopped
2 tablespoons tomato paste
1 teaspoon brown sugar
2 tablespoons white vinegar
½ head cabbage, coarsely chopped
Dollop of sour cream
Freshly minced dill for garnish

Simmer the beef in the water for about 1 hour. Add the salt and pepper. Skim the top until it is clear.

Add the beets, carrots, butter, onion, tomato paste, sugar and vinegar. Simmer, stirring occasionally, for about 15 minutes.

Stir in the cabbage and continue to simmer for 10 more minutes, or until the cabbage is tender. Adjust the seasonings.

Serve in large soup bowls with a generous dollop of sour cream and minced dill for garnish. Borscht may be served hot or cold.

(ELAINE BENSON)

Beet Wine

About 7 28-ounce bottles

8 pounds beets, trimmed
6 quarts water
1 pound raisins
3 oranges, peeled and cut into pieces
6 pounds sugar
1 package active dry yeast

Wash the beets thoroughly. Cut into chunks, leaving the skins on. Boil in 3 quarts of the water until tender, about 20 minutes. Pour the contents through a strainer and cheesecloth into a large nonmetallic container. The juice is all that is used for the wine.

Add the remaining 3 quarts of water and the raisins, oranges, sugar and yeast to the beet juice. Stir well. Cover with a clean towel and stir well every day for 9 days. Bottle and cork lightly. (Soda bottles work well.) Let stand for 2 weeks, until the action stops; then cork tightly.

(THELMA MILNE)

Pickled Beets

2 cups

18 medium-sized fresh beets
¼ cup water
¾ cup white vinegar
6 whole cloves
¼ teaspoon mustard seeds
6 tablespoons sugar, or less according to taste
¼ teaspoon salt
1 small onion, sliced

Cut off the tops of the beets. Wash the beets and cook for approximately 20 minutes. Drain and let cool. Peel and slice them, and set aside.

In a saucepan, combine all the remaining ingredients except the onion and bring to a boil. Add the beets and onion, and boil for 1–2 minutes. Chill.

(LYNN WESNOFSKE)

BROCCOLI

Broccoli and Rice Salad
4–6 servings

2 lemons
4–6 shallots
½ bunch fresh Italian parsley
1 bunch broccoli
1 pint cherry tomatoes
4 cups cooked rice, at room temperature
Salt and freshly ground black pepper to taste
Balsamic vinegar or aged red wine vinegar
Olive oil

Remove the zest from the lemons and chop very fine. Peel and chop shallots very fine. Pull the parsley leaves from the stems and chop fairly fine.

Break the broccoli into small flowerets (about 2 cups) and blanch in boiling salted water for 1–2 minutes. Drain, then plunge into ice-cold water and drain again. Cut the cherry tomatoes in half.

Combine all the ingredients with the rice and dress with salt, pepper, vinegar and olive oil to taste.

(DANA JACOBI)

Chicken and Broccoli Steaks

6 servings

2 pounds chicken breasts, boned and skinned
8 tablespoons butter
¼ cup minced shallots
½ teaspoon paprika
2 tablespoons chopped fresh parsley
1½ cups finely chopped fresh broccoli, cooked
2 eggs, lightly beaten
2 cups fresh bread crumbs
½ cup vegetable oil

Grind the chicken breasts in a food processor or meat grinder and place in a bowl.

Melt 2 tablespoons of the butter in a heavy skillet, add the shallots and sauté for 5 minutes. Remove from the heat and stir in the paprika and parsley. Add the shallot mixture to the chicken, along with 3 tablespoons of the butter and the broccoli. Mix well.

Shape into 6 oval-shaped patties, each about 1 inch thick. Dip each patty in the eggs and coat with the bread crumbs. Heat the remaining 3 tablespoons of butter and the oil in a heavy skillet. Sauté the patties until golden brown on both sides.

(MICHELE EVANS)

Sesame Broccoli

4 servings

1 bunch broccoli
2 tablespoons sesame oil
2 tablespoons tamari sauce
3 tablespoons sesame seeds, toasted

Break up the broccoli into flowerets, peel the stem and cut into 1-inch-long strips the width of a pencil. Blanch the broccoli for 2 minutes, then plunge into ice-cold water to retain the color. Drain well.

Combine the sesame oil and tamari sauce, and toss with the broccoli. Chill well or serve warm. Sprinkle with the sesame seeds before serving.

(BETH LORD)

Tong's Broccoli

4 servings

1 bunch broccoli
2 tablespoons sesame oil
1 clove garlic, minced
1 slice fresh ginger, minced
¼ cup sherry
1 tablespoon soy sauce
¼ cup chicken stock
1 teaspoon cornstarch

Wash the broccoli and break up into flowerets. Slice them in the direction of their growth into thin slices. Peel the heavy stems and slice the interior of the stems diagonally. Dry.

Heat the oil in a heavy skillet, add the garlic and ginger, and cook until brown. Add the broccoli and fry over high heat for 2–3 minutes, stirring constantly. Add the sherry, reduce the heat and cover the pan. Cook for 2 minutes longer.

Uncover the pan and add the combined soy sauce, chicken stock and cornstarch. Continue cooking until the sauce thickens. Serve at once.

(MR. AND MRS. M. E. BARZELAY)

Broccoli Soufflé
4–6 servings

4 cups chopped broccoli flowerets
2 tablespoons butter
2 tablespoons all-purpose flour
½ cup milk
½ cup heavy cream
1 tablespoon freshly grated Parmesan cheese
Pinch of grated nutmeg
Salt and freshly ground black pepper to taste
4 egg yolks
5 egg whites, stiffly beaten

Preheat the oven to 350°. Butter a 2-quart soufflé dish and dust the sides with flour.

Put the broccoli in enough boiling water to cover, boil for 5 minutes, drain well and mince. Drain again.

Melt the butter in a saucepan over low heat. Add the flour and cook for 2–3 minutes, stirring constantly. Do not let the roux brown.

Mix the milk and cream together and stir into the flour mixture. Continue stirring until thickened and smooth. Stir in the cheese, nutmeg, salt and pepper. Remove from the heat and cool slightly.

Place the egg yolks in a bowl and stir in one third of the cream sauce. When thoroughly blended, add the egg-yolk mixture slowly to the rest of the cream sauce, stirring constantly.

Add the broccoli and mix well. Stir in about ⅓ cup of the beaten egg whites, then fold in the rest of the egg whites.

Pour the mixture into the prepared soufflé dish. Place the dish in a pan of hot water, coming halfway up the sides. Bake for 35 minutes, or until the soufflé is well set.

(JULES BOND)

BRUSSELS SPROUTS

Cream of Brussels Sprout Soup

4 servings

3 tablespoons butter
½ cup diced celery
½ cup diced onions
3 tablespoons flour
1 quart chicken broth
1 pound Brussels sprouts, washed,
trimmed and sliced in half
1½ cups heavy cream
½ teaspoon ground nutmeg
Salt and white pepper to taste

Melt the butter in a heavy saucepan over low heat. Add the celery and onion, and sauté until the onion is soft and transparent. Add the flour and continue cooking for 2–3 minutes, stirring constantly. Slowly add the chicken broth, stirring to dissolve the flour. Bring to a boil. Add the Brussels sprouts and cook for about 8 minutes, or until the sprouts are tender.

Pour the soup into a blender or food processor and process until smooth. Return the soup to the saucepan and bring to a boil. Remove from the heat and add the cream, nutmeg, salt and pepper.

(MELISSA LORD)

Sautéed Brussels Sprouts

4–6 servings

1½ pounds Brussels sprouts, washed and trimmed
1 medium onion, chopped
1 whole clove
1 bay leaf
¼ cup butter

Soak the sprouts for 10 minutes in warm lightly salted water, then drain. Combine the sprouts, onion, clove and bay leaf in a saucepan with enough water to just cover the sprouts. Simmer until tender, about 10 minutes. Drain well. Discard clove and bay leaf.

Melt the butter in a heavy skillet over low heat and add the sprouts. Shake the skillet frequently until the sprouts are lightly browned. Serve plain or over rice. Salt and pepper to taste.

(NANCY WASSERMAN)

Sprouts au Gratin

4 servings

1 pound Brussels sprouts, washed and trimmed
4 slices bacon, cut into small pieces
5 tablespoons butter
Salt and freshly ground black pepper to taste
½ cup heavy cream
⅓ cup bread crumbs

Preheat the oven to 400°.

Parboil the sprouts, drain, slice and set aside.

Cook the bacon in 1 tablespoon of the butter in a heavy skillet over low heat until it is limp, not crisp. Add the sprouts, salt and pepper, and cook, stirring, over medium heat for 2 minutes.

Transfer to a buttered gratin dish. Pour the cream on top. Sprinkle with the bread crumbs and dot with the remaining butter. Bake for 25 minutes.

(EDWARD DRAGON)

Gail Besemer's Sprouts

8 servings

2 pounds fresh Brussels sprouts, washed,
　trimmed and halved
½ cup olive oil
4 cloves garlic, crushed
2 sweet red peppers, cut into thin strips
1 tablespoon fresh oregano
¾ pound fresh button mushrooms, wiped and halved
½ cup diced peeled fresh ripe tomatoes
Salt and freshly ground black pepper to taste

Steam the sprouts for 5 minutes. Heat the oil in a heavy skillet over medium heat. Add the garlic, red peppers and oregano, and sauté for 5 minutes. Stir in the sprouts, mushrooms and tomatoes. Cook over low heat for about 10 minutes. Remove from the heat. Season with salt and pepper.

(GAIL PARLATORE)

CABBAGE

John Duck Jr.'s Coleslaw
10 servings

2 heads white cabbage
4 stalks celery
4 carrots
1 green pepper
4 ounces onion
3 cups mayonnaise
Salt, freshly ground black pepper and sugar to taste

The vegetables and mayonnaise should be cold. Wash and clean the vegetables, then grate or finely chop them. Mix them with the cold mayonnaise. Season with salt, pepper and sugar.

(JOHN DUCK JR.'S RESTAURANT)

Herbed Cabbage Medley
4 servings

2 tablespoons butter
1 medium onion, sliced
2 cups shredded cabbage
1 cup shredded carrots
½ teaspoon salt
1 tablespoon chopped fresh oregano

Melt the butter in a heavy skillet over low heat, add the onion and sauté for 5 minutes. Stir in the cabbage, carrots, salt and oregano. Cover and continue cooking over medium heat for 8 minutes. Remove from the heat and serve immediately. Great with fish.

(PEGGY GRIFFIN)

Bubble and Squeak
6 servings

4 cups boiled coarsely shredded cabbage
4 cups mashed potatoes
2 tablespoons chopped fresh parsley
Salt and freshly ground black pepper to taste
1 tablespoon white vinegar
1 tablespoon Worcestershire sauce
4 tablespoons butter

In a mixing bowl, combine all the ingredients except the butter. Form patties from the cabbage-potato mixture.

Melt the butter in a large, heavy skillet. Add the patties, pressing down each patty. When one side has turned a golden brown, turn over and cook the other side. Add more butter if necessary.

("Bubble and Squeak is an old English dish that probably came into being during World War I, when food was hard to get."
—NICHOLAS AND MELISSA SIMUNEK)

Sweet and Sour Red Cabbage

6 servings

1 large head red cabbage
3 tablespoons butter
2 tablespoons chopped onions
2 Macintosh apples, washed, cored and thinly sliced
¼ cup boiling water
1 tablespoon salt
¼ cup red wine
¼ cup brown sugar
½ teaspoon caraway seeds

Remove the outer leaves of the cabbage and discard. Cut the cabbage into wedges and remove the core. Shred the cabbage and soak in cold water. Drain.

Melt the butter in a heavy saucepan and sauté the onion in it for 3 minutes. Add the cabbage. Cover the saucepan and simmer for 10 minutes.

Add the apples, water and salt. Cover and simmer, stirring occasionally, for about 30 minutes, or until the onions, cabbage and apples are tender and all the water has been absorbed.

Add the wine, brown sugar and caraway seeds, and continue simmering for 10 more minutes.

(NANCY WASSERMAN)

Dad's Red Cabbage

8 servings

1 medium head red cabbage
6 tablespoons butter or bacon drippings
1 large onion, thinly sliced
Salt to taste
¼ teaspoon freshly ground black pepper
Crushed red pepper flakes
Boiling water
1 cup dry red wine

Remove the outer leaves of the cabbage and discard. Core and coarsely shred the cabbage.

Melt the butter in a Dutch oven. Add the onion and simmer for several minutes. Add the cabbage, seasonings and enough boiling water to barely cover the cabbage. Cover and bring to a boil. Reduce the heat and simmer slowly for about 1 hour.

Add the wine and continue simmering, uncovered, for 20 minutes, stirring occasionally.

("My father's parents made this on their farm in Croatia. They grew their own food and made their own wine." —**BARBARA NIKOLICH**)

Stuffed Cabbage

6–8 servings

2 medium cabbages
2 pounds ground beef
1 cup raw brown rice
2 eggs, beaten
Salt and freshly ground black pepper to taste
2 onions, chopped
2½ pounds ripe tomatoes, finely chopped
¾ cup or more beef broth
2 bay leaves
2 onions, peeled and pierced with cloves
18 ginger snaps, crushed
4 tablespoons freshly squeezed lemon juice
4 tablespoons brown sugar
1 cup currants or raisins

Cut a circle around the core of each cabbage and loosen the leaves. Drop the leaves into a large pot of boiling salted water. Lift out after 3–4 minutes. Lay out the large outer leaves flat. Cut out a small V from the root end to remove the hard spine.

Combine the beef, rice, eggs, salt, pepper and chopped onions in a large bowl. Blend well. Place about 2 tablespoons of filling onto each leaf and roll, tucking the sides in first to form a firm envelope.

Arrange the rolled leaves in layers in a Dutch oven. Smother with the tomatoes and enough beef broth to cover. Add the bay leaves and onions with cloves. Simmer for 1 hour on top of the stove.

Add the ginger snaps, lemon juice, brown sugar and currants. Simmer for 15 more minutes, stirring occasionally. Remove from the heat and serve.

(MYRNA DAVIS)

Red Cabbage with Apples

2–3 slices bacon
1 head red cabbage, shredded
1 tablespoon brown sugar
2 teaspoons grated onions
Salt and freshly ground black pepper to taste
6 tart apples, peeled, cored and sliced
½ cup white vinegar
½ cup water

Fry the bacon in a large, heavy skillet until crisp. Add the cabbage and steam over low heat. Add the remaining ingredients, cover and cook over low heat until the cabbage is tender.

(MRS. RALPH SMYLE)

Red Cabbage and Chestnuts

6 servings

16 chestnuts
6 strips bacon
1 small head red cabbage, shredded
1 cup red wine
Salt and freshly ground black pepper to taste

Make an incision around the crown of each chestnut. Cover the chestnuts with water, bring to a boil and cook for 20 minutes. Drain, then peel the chestnuts.

Fry the bacon in a heavy skillet and, when half-cooked, add the cabbage. When the cabbage is limp, add the chestnuts, wine, salt and pepper. Reduce the heat, cover and simmer for 1½ hours. A wonderful accompaniment to roast duck.

(JUDITH SCHUB)

CAULIFLOWER

Cream of Cauliflower Soup
6 servings

3 large leeks
2 tablespoons butter
1 cup diced celery heart
1 medium onion, diced
1 quart chicken broth
1 medium cauliflower, broken into flowerets
1 cup light cream
Salt and freshly ground black pepper to taste
Toasted slivered almonds for garnish

Cut off the roots of the leeks, as well as the green parts at the point where they begin to pale. Split the leeks lengthwise and rinse thoroughly. Cut into ½-inch slices.

Melt the butter over medium heat in a 3-quart saucepan. Add the leeks, celery and onion, and cook gently, stirring occasionally, until the vegetables are tender, about 8 minutes. Add the chicken broth and cauliflower, and simmer, covered, until the cauliflower is soft, about 15 minutes.

Purée the mixture through the fine disk of a food mill. Return the purée to the saucepan and add the cream, salt and pepper. Heat to serving temperature but do not allow to boil. Ladle into bowls and garnish with slivered almonds.

(HELEN GREEN)

Baked Cheese Cauliflower
4–6 servings

5 tablespoons butter
½ cup chopped green peppers
1 tablespoon all-purpose flour
½ cup white wine
½ cup milk
1 tablespoon caraway seeds
1 cup grated Gruyère or sharp cheddar cheese
1 head cauliflower, broken into flowerets

Preheat the oven to 400°.

Melt 2 tablespoons of the butter in a heavy skillet, add the green peppers and sauté until crisp-tender.

Add the remaining butter and the flour, wine, milk, caraway seeds and grated cheese. Continue cooking, stirring constantly, until the mixture has the texture of a cream sauce.

Place the cauliflowerets in a baking dish and pour the sauce over them. Cover and bake for 30–40 minutes, or until the cauliflower is tender.

(MRS. THOMAS FOGARTY)

Three-Vegetable Purée

8–10 servings

1 pound carrots, peeled
1 head cauliflower, separated into flowerets
1 bunch broccoli, cut into 2-inch pieces with stalks peeled
1 cup heavy cream
1½ sticks sweet butter
Salt and freshly ground black pepper to taste
3 large eggs

Preheat the oven to 375°. Butter 8–10 ramekins.

Steam the vegetables separately until they are very tender. Drain. Purée each vegetable in a blender or food processor, adding ⅓ cup of the cream and 3 tablespoons melted butter to each batch. Season with salt and pepper. Add 1 egg to each vegetable while processing.

Using a spatula or spoon, place the purées, one at a time, in the ramekins. Try to have each layer as flat as possible and equally thick. Place the molds in a pan of water and cover with waxed paper rubbed with butter. Bake for 1 hour. Run knife around the edge of the ramekins and unmold onto plate.

(**DAVID ZIFF**, COOKING, INC.)

Pickled Cauliflower

About 6 pints, depending on size of cauliflower

1 quart white distilled vinegar
2 tablespoons mustard seeds
1 cup sugar
8 whole cloves
4 sticks cinnamon
2 heads cauliflower

Combine all the ingredients except the cauliflower and simmer for 15 minutes.

Wash the cauliflower, cut away the leaves and tough stems, and break into uniform flowerets. Blanch them in boiling water for 2 minutes. Drain and place in sterilized jars.

Strain the spices from the vinegar and pour the liquid over the cauliflower. Leave ½-inch space at the top. Seal and process the jars for 10 minutes in boiling water. Allow to age several days before using.

(POLLY STARK)

CELERIAC

Celery Root Soup
4 servings

1 large celery root (celeriac)
3–4 tablespoons safflower oil
6 medium carrots, sliced
1 large onion, chopped
4 cloves garlic, minced
½ cup finely chopped leeks (white part only)
4 cups chicken broth
½ cup chopped celery leaves
1 cup chopped fresh parsley
2 tablespoons finely chopped fresh basil
1 teaspoon fresh thyme
1 teaspoon fresh oregano
1 teaspoon curry powder
2 tablespoons freshly squeezed lemon juice

Clean, peel and dice the celery root.

Heat the oil in a large, heavy saucepan over medium heat. Add the celery root, carrots, onion, garlic and leeks. Cover and cook, stirring occasionally, until the vegetables are soft, about 12–15 minutes.

Add the chicken broth, celery leaves, parsley, basil, thyme and oregano. Simmer, covered, for 45 minutes, stirring occasionally. Stir in the curry powder and lemon juice. Remove from the heat. This is a hearty autumn soup that is at its best when served with fresh sourdough bread.

(SUE HOLZMAN)

Root Soup with Pasta and Goat Cheese

4–6 servings

2 tablespoons olive oil
1 medium onion, chopped
1 carrot
1 medium kohlrabi
1 small celery root (celeriac)
1 small white turnip
6 cups water or chicken broth
2–3 medium tomatoes
2 tablespoons concentrated tomato purée (in tube)
1 cup tortellini
2 medium-sized pieces of goat cheese marinated in olive
   oil and herbs and crumbled

Heat the oil in the bottom of a large pot over medium heat. Add the onion and sauté until soft and transparent.

Peel and cut the carrot, kohlrabi, celery root and turnip into ⅜-inch cubes. Add to the pot. Pour in the water or chicken broth and bring to a boil. Reduce the heat and simmer gently, uncovered, for about 15 minutes.

Peel and seed the tomatoes. Cut into ⅜-inch cubes and add to the soup while it is cooking. Add the tomato concentrate and pasta, stirring well. Cook until the pasta is *al dente,* tender but firm.

Remove from the heat. Just before serving, top each bowl with some goat cheese.

(DANA JACOBI)

Celeriac and Potato Purée

6 servings

1 pound celery root (celeriac)
1¼ cups chicken broth
Butter, salt and freshly ground black pepper to taste
5–6 cups well-seasoned mashed potatoes

Peel and cube the celeriac. Place in a saucepan and add the chicken broth. Bring to a boil and simmer until quite tender, about 6 minutes. Drain, then purée in a food mill. Add butter, salt and pepper.

Using a fork, mix the purée with the mashed potatoes and serve hot.

(HELEN GREEN)

Braised Celeriac

4 servings

3 medium celery roots (celeriac)
Butter for greasing saucepan
⅓ cup butter, cut into small pieces
Juice of ½ lemon
½ teaspoon salt
¼ teaspoon sugar
1 cup chicken broth

Scrub the celeriacs and slice into rounds about ½ inch thick.

Butter the bottom of a heavy saucepan. Put in the sliced celeriacs. Add the butter pieces, lemon juice, salt, sugar and broth. Simmer for ½ hour, or until tender.

(CAROL WILLIAMS)

Creamed Celery Root

6 servings

3 pounds peeled and cubed celery root (celeriac)
2 quarts water
1 tablespoon plus 2 teaspoons freshly squeezed
  lemon juice
4 tablespoons butter
1 medium onion, finely chopped
4 shallots, minced
½ cup heavy cream
2 tablespoons finely chopped fresh coriander
Salt and white pepper to taste

In a saucepan, combine the celery root and water. Add the 1 tablespoon of lemon juice, cover and bring to a boil. Uncover and simmer until tender, about 6 minutes. Drain and set aside.

Melt the butter in a heavy skillet over medium heat. Add the onion and shallots, and sauté until transparent, about 5 minutes. Process the celery root and butter mixture in a food processor and gradually add the cream; purée until smooth.

Place the mixture in a bowl and stir in the 2 teaspoons of lemon juice, the fresh coriander, and the salt and pepper. Mix well and serve immediately.

FENNEL

Fenouil Braisé
4–8 servings

4 nice-sized unblemished fennel bulbs
7 tablespoons butter
1½ cups chicken broth
Salt and freshly ground black pepper to taste
1½ cups grated Gruyère or Swiss cheese

Preheat the oven to 400°.

Pull off the outer leaves of the fennel bulbs if they seem tough and discard. Wash each bulb well and cut in half.

Layer the pieces cut side down in a casserole. Dot with 3 tablespoons of the butter. Add the chicken broth, salt and pepper, and bring to a boil on top of the stove. Cover tightly and place the casserole in the oven. Bake for about 25–30 minutes, or until tender but firm. The fennel must not become mushy. Drain.

Cut each piece in half and arrange the quarters cut side up in one layer in a baking dish. Sprinkle with the cheese. Melt the remaining 4 tablespoons of butter and pour over all. Bake for 10 minutes, then place the dish under the broiler until the cheese becomes golden brown.

(CRAIG CLAIBORNE)

Fennel with Orange Sauce

4 servings

1 pound fennel bulbs
2½ tablespoons butter
2 tablespoons finely chopped shallots
2 teaspoons all-purpose flour
½ cup freshly squeezed orange juice
Grated rind of 2 oranges

Trim the fennel bulbs and cut in half. Cook in boiling salted water until just tender, about 10 minutes. Set aside.

Melt 1 tablespoon of the butter in a heavy skillet over medium heat, add the shallots and sauté until transparent, about 2 minutes.

Melt the remaining butter in a saucepan, add the flour and stir until thick. Pour in the orange juice and continue stirring over low heat until the sauce boils and thickens. Stir in the orange rind and shallots.

Drain the fennel and arrange the pieces cut side up. Spoon the sauce over the pieces, opening the leaves of the fennel to allow the sauce to penetrate. Serve immediately.

AUTUMN FRUITS

Apple Crisp
8 servings

8 greening apples
Juice of 1 lemon
½ cup white sugar
1 teaspoon ground cinnamon
¾ cup all-purpose flour
½ cup brown sugar
¼ pound (8 tablespoons) sweet butter
Fresh whipped cream

Preheat the oven to 350°.

Peel, core and slice the apples. They should make about 5 cups of slices. Drizzle the lemon juice over them. Mix the white sugar and apples together and place in an 8½ × 12½-inch pan. Sprinkle with cinnamon.

Combine the flour and brown sugar; cut in the butter. Cover the apples with this mixture. Bake for 40 minutes, or until the topping is golden brown. Great with fresh whipped cream.

(**SHELLEY MODLIN**)

Open-Faced Apple Pie

8 servings

CRUST

1½ cups flour
¾ teaspoon salt
½ cup lard
4 tablespoons water
1 tablespoon butter, at room temperature

FILLING

2½ pounds tart cooking apples
¾ cup sugar
1 teaspoon ground cinnamon
4 egg yolks
½ cup heavy cream
1 teaspoon vanilla extract

Preheat the oven to 350°.

Combine the flour and salt in a mixing bowl. Cut in the lard until the bits of lard are the size of peas. Blend in the water.

On a lightly floured surface, roll out the pastry into an 11-inch circle, rolling with light strokes. Fold the pastry in half and lift to the center of a 9-inch-deep pie pan. Unfold and fit carefully. Fold the edges 1 inch high and flute the rim. Spread the butter on the bottom of the shell. Refrigerate.

Pare and core the apples, and slice into eighths. Arrange the slices in the pie shell in an attractive pattern. Sprinkle with ½ cup of the sugar and the cinnamon. Bake for 30 minutes.

In a small bowl, beat together the egg yolks, the cream, the remaining sugar and the vanilla.

Remove the pie from the oven, pour the egg-yolk mixture over the apples and return to the oven. Bake for 35 minutes, or until the apples are tender and the topping turns golden brown. Serve slightly warm.

("This was my mother's recipe and my favorite childhood dessert. The custard topping makes it special." —**EDNA BARTHAU**)

Cider Pie

6–8 servings

1½ cups sweet apple cider
1 cup light-brown sugar
2 tablespoons sweet butter
¼ teaspoon salt
3 eggs
9-inch pastry shell
Nutmeg

Preheat the oven to 325°.

Boil the cider in a saucepan until it is reduced to ¾ cup, approximately 10 minutes. Remove from the heat. Add the sugar, butter and salt. Stir until the sugar is dissolved and the butter melted. If necessary, return to the heat but do not let boil.

Beat the eggs well. Pour a little cider mixture into the beaten eggs, stirring constantly. Add the remaining cider mixture to the egg mixture. Mix thoroughly.

Pour the filling into the pastry shell and sprinkle with nutmeg. Bake for 30–35 minutes, or until a knife inserted into the center comes out clean. Cool thoroughly before serving.

(**SUSAN YOUNG**)

Raw Apple Cake
6–8 servings

2 eggs
2 cups sugar
1¼ cups oil
⅓ cup milk
1 teaspoon vanilla extract
2½ cups all-purpose flour
½ teaspoon salt
1 teaspoon baking soda
1 teaspoon ground cinnamon
2½ cups chopped peeled apples
1 cup chopped nuts
1 cup raisins

Preheat the oven to 350°.

Mix together the first 5 ingredients in a large mixing bowl.

Sift together the dry ingredients and stir into the egg mixture. Blend thoroughly.

Stir in the apples, nuts and raisins. Mix well.

Pour into an ungreased 13 × 9 × 2-inch baking pan and bake for 35–40 minutes, or until a knife inserted into the center comes out clean.

(SUSAN YOUNG)

Cranapple Walnut Cake

12 servings

1¾ *cups light brown sugar*
½ *cup vegetable oil*
2 *eggs, beaten*
1 *teaspoon vanilla extract*
1 *cup white flour*
1 *cup whole wheat flour*
1 *teaspoon baking soda*
1 *teaspoon ground cinnamon*
½ *teaspoon ground nutmeg*
1 *teaspoon salt*
2 *cups diced peeled apples*
½ *cup chopped walnuts*
2⅔ *cups fresh cranberries*

Preheat the oven to 350°.

Cream together the sugar and oil in a mixing bowl. Stir in the eggs and vanilla. Blend well and set aside.

Sift together the flours, baking soda, cinnamon, nutmeg and salt. Slowly add the dry mixture to the egg mixture.

When thoroughly blended, stir in the apples, walnuts and cranberries. Mix well.

Spread the batter into a well-greased 9 × 13-inch pan and bake for 45–50 minutes, or until a knife inserted into the center comes out clean.

(CATHY SANTACROSS)

Walnut Special Cake
12 servings

CAKE
1 pound shelled walnuts
1 6-ounce box zwieback
1 teaspoon baking powder
½ teaspoon salt
12 eggs, separated
1 box confectioners' sugar
1 teaspoon almond extract
2 tablespoons Cognac or brandy

FROSTING
¾ pound butter, softened
1 box confectioners' sugar
6 egg yolks
¼ cup heavy cream
2 jiggers Cognac
1 teaspoon almond extract
2 tablespoons cocoa
1 teaspoon instant coffee

Preheat the oven to 325°.

Grind the walnuts and zwieback together. Stir in the baking powder and salt. Set aside.

Combine the egg yolks, sugar, almond extract and Cognac. Blend well. Stir into the nut mixture.

Beat the egg whites until stiff and fold into the batter. When well blended, pour the batter into 3 buttered and floured 8-inch round cake pans. Bake for 25 minutes, or until a knife inserted into the center comes out clean.

To make the frosting, cream together the butter and sugar. Stir in the egg yolks, one at a time, until well blended. Stir in the heavy cream, Cognac, almond extract, cocoa and coffee. Blend well.

Frost the cake when well cooled. A truly elegant, rich and sinful dessert.

("I dedicate this to Theresa and Bridey, who have given me all my best recipes."—**NANCY BANGERT**)

Warm Pear Dessert
4–6 servings

4 fresh pears, cored and sliced
1 cup flour
½ cup sugar
½ cup sweet butter
Nutmeg

Preheat the oven to 375°.

Place the pears in a shallow baking dish. Mix the flour and sugar together, then cut in the butter. Spread the mixture over the pears and sprinkle with nutmeg. Bake for 35 minutes. Cool for 5 minutes.

(**MARY GABBARD**)

Pear Butter

4 ½-pint jars

4½ pounds Bosc pears, peeled, cored and sliced
½–1 cup sugar
Grated zest of 1 lemon

Purée the pears in a food processor fitted with a steel chopping blade. Place the pears and ½ cup of sugar in a stainless-steel or enamel-lined pot. Bring to a boil and reduce the heat so the pears are gently simmering.

Taste to see if the mixture is sweet enough for your taste, keeping in mind that the sugar should enhance the natural pear flavor without overwhelming it. Add more sugar if desired, up to 1 cup, and continue cooking, stirring frequently to prevent the pears from sticking to the bottom of the pot. Use a long-handled wooden spoon, which will not scratch the bottom of the pot. Be careful when stirring, as the mixture has a tendency to splatter. The butter is done when it clings to the spoon when the spoon is turned upside down. Add the lemon and stir well.

Immediately put the pear butter into sterilized jars, being careful to eliminate air pockets, and seal. Process in boiling-water bath for 10 minutes according to the jar manufacturer's directions.

(DANA JACOBI)

GREENS:
MUSTARD SPINACH, SWISS CHARD AND KALE

Mustard Spinach Stroganoff
4 servings

1 pound mustard spinach
½ cup sour cream
⅓ cup chopped scallions (green and white parts)
½ teaspoon dry mustard
Nutmeg grating
1 tablespoon dry sherry
½ pound mushrooms, wiped clean, sliced and
    browned in butter

Clean the mustard spinach and chop coarsely into approximately 2-inch lengths. Steam until wilted. Drain well.

Combine the sour cream, scallions, dry mustard, nutmeg and sherry in a saucepan. Heat over very low flame. Add the spinach and mushrooms, and mix well. Serve immediately.

(RUTH COBBETT BIEMILLER)

Swiss Chard
6 servings

36 Swiss chard leaves
2 tablespoons olive oil
3 cloves garlic, finely chopped
2 tablespoons butter
1 cup freshly grated Parmesan cheese
Salt to taste

Preheat the oven to 400°.

Cut the chard leaves away from the stalks. Wash the leaves and the stalks. Heat the oil in a heavy saucepan over medium heat, add the leaves and garlic, and sauté until the leaves are wilted. Pass through a food mill. Set aside.

Cut the stalks into 3-inch lengths and drop in boiling salted water. Cook until just tender, about 25 minutes. Drain.

Cover the bottom of a buttered dish with the chopped leaves. Layer the stalks on top of the leaves. Layer thin slices of butter next. Sprinkle with the cheese. Season with salt. Bake for 15 minutes.

(HAROLD EDELMAN)

Baked Kale

6–8 servings

2½ pounds fresh kale, stems removed
4 tablespoons sweet butter
3 tablespoons all-purpose flour
1 cup milk
⅓ cup grated Jarlsberg cheese
Salt and freshly ground black pepper to taste
¼ teaspoon freshly grated nutmeg
½ cup grated Jarlsberg cheese

Preheat the oven to 425°.

Rinse the kale. Steam it in a covered Dutch oven until wilted, 6–8 minutes. Drain and press the leaves to remove as much liquid as possible. Chop fine and set aside.

Melt the butter in a small saucepan over medium heat; remove from the heat and whisk in the flour. Return to the heat and stir constantly for 2 minutes. Whisk in the milk and continue cooking until the mixture thickens and bubbles, about 1 minute. Remove from the heat; stir in the ⅓ cup of cheese, salt, pepper and nutmeg. Melt the remaining tablespoon of butter in a small saucepan and set aside.

Combine the kale and the sauce and pour into a well-buttered 1½-quart baking dish. Sprinkle with the ½ cup grated Jarlsberg. Bake until golden and bubbly, 10–15 minutes.

LEEKS

October Stew

10 servings

6 tablespoons peanut oil
¼ cup butter
2 cups diced peeled parsnips
1½ cups diced peeled golden beets
4 cups diced peeled turnips
1 teaspoon salt
5 cups chopped leeks (white part only)
½ cup finely chopped fresh thyme
1 teaspoon ground fennel seed
4 cups firmly packed chopped fresh Swiss chard
2½ cups cooked cranberry beans
2½ quarts water
5 tablespoons miso
½ cup hot water
Salt and freshly ground black pepper to taste

Heat the oil and butter in a large, heavy pot over medium heat until the butter is melted. Add the parsnips, beets, turnips, and salt, and sauté for 15 minutes, stirring occasionally.

Stir in the leeks, thyme and fennel and continue to sauté, for another 15 minutes, stirring occasionally. Add the Swiss chard, beans and water.

Dissolve the miso in the ½ cup of hot water and stir into the soup. Cover, bring to a boil, reduce the heat and simmer for at least ½ hour. Season with salt and pepper. Ladle into warm soup bowls and serve.

(ROBERT CHAPMAN)

Leek Salad

2 servings

4 leeks, washed well (white part only)
½ cup light wine vinegar, chilled
½ cup imported olive oil
Salt and freshly ground black pepper to taste
¼ teaspoon sugar
Bibb lettuce leaves

Cut the leeks crosswise into 1½-inch pieces and cook in boiling salted water. Drain, cover and cool in the refrigerator.

One hour before serving, combine the vinegar, oil, salt, pepper and sugar. Place the leeks on a bed of Bibb lettuce and pour the dressing over them.

(PEGGY FITZPATRICK)

Leek-Saffron Soup

4 servings

4 tablespoons butter
1 cup diced unpeeled potatoes
4 cups halved and thinly sliced leeks (white part only)
2 tablespoons flour
1½ cups milk
1 cup water
2 generous pinches of saffron strands, soaked in a little
   water for 10 minutes to soften
1 cup coarsely chopped ripe tomatoes
Salt and freshly ground black pepper to taste
Fresh parsley for garnish

Melt the butter in a heavy saucepan over low heat. Add the potatoes and cook until tender but not brown.

Stir in the leeks and continue cooking for 10 minutes, allowing the vegetables to stew. Sprinkle in the flour, stirring well, and then pour in the milk and water. Bring the soup to the boil, stirring frequently. Add the saffron in its soaking water, lower the heat and let the soup simmer for about 15 minutes.

Meanwhile, cook the tomatoes down to a pulp over low heat, adding a little water if necessary. Strain the pulp (to remove the skins and seeds) and purée in a blender or food processor.

Season the soup with salt and pepper, and ladle into individual soup bowls. Swirl the tomato purée into each bowl, garnish with parsley and serve.

Leek and Fish Pie

6 servings

2 tablespoons butter
4–6 leeks, trimmed, washed and sliced into 1-inch pieces
  (approximately 6 cups)
Salt and freshly ground black pepper to taste
Fresh tarragon
1½ pounds fresh codfish (blackfish, tilefish and scrod are
  also good)
2 tablespoons chopped fresh dill
2 tablespoons chopped fresh parsley
1 teaspoon fresh thyme
1 cup Basic White Sauce (recipe follows), with dash of
  Tabasco
Rich pie crust top

Preheat the oven to 350°.

Melt the butter in a heavy skillet over medium heat. Add the leeks and sauté until soft, about 15 minutes. Place the leeks in the bottom of a buttered pie dish. Sprinkle with salt, pepper and tarragon. Set aside.

Steam the fish until it flakes, then arrange it over the leeks. Sprinkle with a mixture of dill, parsley and thyme. Pour the white sauce over all. Top with pie crust and prick with a fork. Bake until the crust is golden brown, about 30 minutes.

BASIC WHITE SAUCE

2 tablespoons butter
2 tablespoons all-purpose flour
¼ teaspoon salt
⅛ teaspoon freshly ground black pepper
1 cup milk

Melt the butter in a saucepan over low heat. Blend in the flour, salt and pepper. Cook over low heat, stirring constantly, until smooth and bubbly.

Remove from the heat. Stir in the milk. Heat to a boil, stirring constantly. Boil, stirring, for 1 minute.

(RUTH COBBETT BIEMILLER)

Stir-Fried Mushrooms and Leeks

4 servings

½ pound leeks, washed and cut into 1-inch lengths
(white part only)
3 tablespoons vegetable oil
2 cups sliced fresh mushrooms
1 tablespoon tamari or soy sauce
2 cloves garlic, halved
½ pound tofu, cut into bite-sized pieces
Parsley for garnish

Cook the leeks in 1 tablespoon of the oil in a heavy skillet or wok over moderate heat for a few minutes. When they begin to soften, add the mushrooms and tamari sauce, and continue stir-frying until the mushrooms are cooked. Remove from the pan and keep warm.

Heat the remaining oil, add the garlic and brown. Remove the garlic and discard. Add the tofu and cook over medium heat until crisp and golden brown on both sides.

Arrange the leek-mushroom mixture and tofu on a warm plate and garnish with parsley before serving.

Vegetable Terrine with Sauce Aurore

8 servings

9 quarts water
6 teaspoons salt
1 pound cabbage, cored and quartered
1½ pounds leeks
2 pounds fresh spinach, washed and stems removed
2 tablespoons butter
1 medium onion, minced
Salt and freshly ground black pepper to taste
Pinch of nutmeg
4 eggs
1 cup heavy cream
Sauce Aurore (recipe follows)
3 tablespoons Gruyère cheese

Preheat the oven to 375°. Butter a long loaf (1½ quart) pan and line the bottom and sides with buttered waxed paper.

Bring 3 quarts of water to a boil with 2 teaspoons of salt in each of 3 separate saucepans. Add the cabbage to the first saucepan and boil for 25 minutes. Drain, rinse in cold water and squeeze dry.

Cut off the green tops of the leeks and discard. Halve the leeks lengthwise and wash well. Boil for 15 minutes in the second saucepan of water. Drain, rinse quickly in cold water and squeeze dry.

Blanch the spinach for 2 minutes in the third saucepan of water. Drain, rinse quickly in cold water and squeeze dry.

Squeeze all the vegetables once again to remove any excess moisture. Chop to medium-coarse texture using a large knife; do not use a food processor, since the texture will be too fine and watery. You should have 1½ cups of each vegetable. Combine and set aside.

Heat the butter in a skillet, add the onion and sauté until soft and transparent. Add the vegetables and sauté gently, stirring constantly, until all the excess liquid is removed, about 10 minutes. Season with salt, pepper and nutmeg. Remove from the heat and set aside.

Beat the eggs with the cream and add to the skillet. Blend well. Taste and adjust seasonings.

Turn the mixture into the prepared pan and cover with the waxed paper. Place the pan in a larger pan and add enough water to come halfway up the sides of the loaf pan. Bake until the custard is set, about 1 hour.

Remove the loaf from the water bath. Run a thin knife blade around the edges, then cool in the pan for 10 minutes. Unmold onto an ovenproof platter and blot dry with paper towels.

Preheat the broiler. Spoon one half of the Sauce Aurore over the loaf. Sprinkle with the cheese.

Broil for several minutes, until the cheese bubbles and is golden. Slice the loaf into pieces about ½ inch thick. Serve with the remaining sauce.

SAUCE AURORE

1 cup heavy cream
1 cup Fresh Tomato Sauce (see page 180)

Reduce the cream in a saucepan over medium heat to ½ cup. Add the tomato sauce and blend well. Stir constantly, allowing the sauce to just reach the boiling point. Serve hot or at room temperature.

(MRS. MARILYN KOCH)

POTATOES

Potato-Apple Salad
4 servings

2 medium potatoes, cooked and cut into chunks
1 apple, cut into small pieces
¼ cup thinly sliced celery
½ cup sunflower seeds
¼ cup minced onions
⅓ cup mayonnaise
⅓ cup sour cream or yogurt
2 tablespoons freshly grated Parmesan cheese
1 tablespoon horseradish
2 teaspoons honey
1 tablespoon olive oil
½ teaspoon salt

The potatoes and apples can be peeled or unpeeled, depending on individual preference. Combine all the ingredients and mix thoroughly.

(SUSAN BROOKS)

Potato Soup

4–6 servings

2 pounds potatoes
3 tablespoons butter
2 tablespoons all-purpose flour
1 tablespoon white vinegar
1 cup sour cream
Fresh parsley or dill for garnish

Peel the potatoes and cut into ½-inch cubes. Place in enough boiling salted water to cover and cook until tender, about 15 minutes. Remove from water and set aside. Mash slightly if a smoother texture is desired. Reserve some of the liquid.

Meanwhile, melt the butter in a saucepan over low heat. Add the flour and cook for about 2 minutes. Add some of the potato liquid, stirring constantly until it thickens to the desired consistency. Add the potato mixture to the thickened liquid and simmer for 5 minutes.

Stir in the vinegar and sour cream. Continue simmering until well blended. Garnish with parsley or dill.

(POLLY STARK)

Minestrone alla Genovese

4–6 servings

2 tablespoons butter
2 tablespoons imported olive oil
2 carrots, scraped and sliced
4 potatoes, chopped
2 small zucchini, chopped
2 stalks celery, chopped
1 cup chopped spinach
5–6 tablespoons fresh peas, optional
12 ounce-can red kidney beans, drained
1 vegetable bouillon cube
6 cups water
5 tablespoons Pesto (see p. 110)
4 cups small pasta, uncooked
Freshly grated Parmesan cheese
Salt and pepper to taste

In a large saucepan, combine the first 11 ingredients and bring to a boil. Reduce the heat, cover and cook for 1½ hours, adding more water if needed and stirring occasionally.

Ten minutes before the minestrone is ready, add the pesto and uncooked pasta, and continue to cook until the pasta reaches the desired tenderness. Serve with Parmesan cheese.

(MYRA WEISER)

Potato Latkes

6 servings

6 medium potatoes, washed and peeled
1 medium onion
1 egg, beaten
1 heaping teaspoon baking powder
Salt and freshly ground black pepper to taste
¾ cup bread crumbs, approximately
Oil for sautéing

Grate the potatoes and onion, partially drain and place in a mixing bowl. Stir in the egg, baking powder, salt and pepper. When thoroughly blended, add enough bread crumbs to make the mixture loose but not watery.

Heat some oil in a heavy skillet (the oil should be at least ½ inch deep). Use a tablespoonful of mixture for canapé-sized latke or a large mixing spoon for regular-sized latke. Add one spoonful to the skillet. Cook gently until golden brown on the bottom. Turn and brown the other side. Remove from the skillet. Continue cooking the latkes until the mixture is used up, adding more oil as needed. Serve immediately with applesauce or sour cream.

(MRS. DIANE JACOBSON)

Masala Fish

4 servings

2 pounds weakfish
4 potatoes, peeled and sliced into chunks
1 red hot pepper, finely sliced
Pinch of salt
2 cups water
2 tablespoons curry powder
1 tablespoon soy sauce

Cut the fish into 1½ × 1½-inch pieces. Combine the potatoes, pepper, salt and water, and bring to a boil.

When the potatoes begin to soften, add the weakfish and curry powder. If necessary, add more water to the desired consistency. Cook for about 15 minutes, taking care not to stir too much, as the fish will fall apart completely.

Add the soy sauce as the finishing touch. Serve with brown rice.

(ANELLE VENVEIJ-LICHTWELD)

Saucisse Paysanne

6 servings

4 medium potatoes, peeled and sliced into
    1-inch-thick pieces
2 small white turnips, peeled and sliced into
    1-inch-thick pieces
4 small white onions, sliced
4 leeks, sliced (white part only)
3 stalks celery, sliced
3 carrots, scraped and sliced
2 cups chopped ripe tomatoes
1 teaspoon chopped fresh thyme
1 bay leaf
¼ cup chopped fresh parsley
Salt and freshly ground black pepper to taste
¼ cup consommé
1 pound Polish sausage

In a large pot, combine all the ingredients except the consommé and sausage. Add enough water to cover, bring to a boil
and cook for 5 minutes.

    Add the consommé and sausage, reduce the heat to a sim-
mer and continue cooking, covered, for 1 hour.

(MRS. HELMUTH KLUGLEIN)

Spicy Oven Fries

6 servings

3 pounds potatoes, unpeeled
3 tablespoons vegetable oil
1 teaspoon salt
½ teaspoon fresh oregano
½ teaspoon paprika
¼ teaspoon crushed garlic
¼ teaspoon freshly ground black pepper
¼ cup freshly grated Parmesan cheese

Preheat the oven to 450°. Oil a 10 × 15-inch baking pan.

Wash the potatoes and cut each one into 8–16 wedges, depending on the size. Drain. Place in a bowl and sprinkle with the oil, tossing lightly.

Combine the remaining ingredients. Sprinkle half of the spice-cheese mixture over the potatoes and toss gently. Sprinkle the rest of the mixture and toss again.

Arrange a single layer of the potatoes in the prepared pan. Bake for 25–30 minutes, loosening the potatoes occasionally.

(MARIE INGRAM)

Mousseline Potatoes

4 servings

2 pounds mealy potatoes, washed and unpeeled
4 egg yolks
½ cup butter, softened
Salt and freshly ground black pepper to taste
6 tablespoons heavy cream
4 tablespoons melted butter

Preheat the oven to 400°.

Boil the potatoes until soft, then peel them and put them through a potato ricer, food mill or strainer.

Using a wire whisk, stir in the egg yolks and butter. Season with salt and pepper. Add enough cream to make the potatoes soft and creamy but still thick enough to hold a shape.

Mound the potatoes into dome shapes and place in a buttered baking dish. Brush with the melted butter and bake for about 10 minutes, or until golden brown.

(JULES BOND)

Cloverleaf Dinner Rolls
24 rolls

1 package active dry yeast
½ cup lukewarm water
⅔ cup shortening
½ cup sugar
2 teaspoons salt
2 eggs, beaten
1 cup mashed potatoes
1 cup scalded milk, cooled
5 cups flour, approximately
Melted butter

Dissolve the yeast in the water.

Combine the shortening, sugar, salt, eggs, potatoes and milk in a large mixing bowl. When thoroughly blended, add the yeast mixture. Stir in the flour and mix well.

Turn the dough out onto a floured board and knead until smooth, about 10 minutes. Roll the dough into 1-inch balls and place 3 balls in each greased muffin cup. Use shortening, not flour, to form the rolls. Brush the tops with melted butter. Let rise in a warm room for 1½–2 hours, or until doubled in bulk.

Preheat the oven to 400°. Bake for about 10 minutes.

(**DORIS FOSTER**)

PUMPKINS

Potage au Potiron (Pumpkin Soup)
6 servings

4 tablespoons butter
3 cups chopped fresh pumpkin meat
1²⁄₃ cups chopped ripe tomatoes
2 quarts boiling water
1 tablespoon rice
2 cups sliced potatoes
Salt and freshly ground black pepper to taste
1 tablespoon basic crème fraîche *(see page 120)*

Heat the butter in a large saucepan. Add the pumpkin and
tomatoes, and cook over low heat for approximately 5 minutes.
Do not brown.

Add the boiling water, rice and potatoes. Simmer for 1 hour
over low heat.

Pour the soup into a blender or food processor and process
until smooth. Season with salt and pepper. Add the cream to
the soup just before serving.

(LA MAISON DES CHAMPS)

Gene Boucher's Pumpkin Stew

16 servings

3 tablespoons oil
6 pounds stewing beef, cut into bite-sized pieces
1½ cups chopped onions
4 bay leaves
2 cloves garlic, crushed
2 teaspoons salt
½ teaspoon freshly ground black pepper
6 medium tomatoes
2–3 cans beef consommé
2 pumpkins (a small pie pumpkin to chop for stew—it
*   should make 3 cups—and one large attractive specimen*
*   to use as a serving container)*
1½ cups diced white potatoes
1½ cup diced turnips
1 cup dried apricots, cut into small pieces and soaked in
*   water until ready for use*
1 cup pitted prunes, cut into small pieces and soaked in
*   water until ready for use*
1 cup raisins, soaked in water until ready for use
4 cups chopped fresh parsley (without stems)
1 pound green beans, cut into 1-inch pieces

Preheat the oven to 300°.

Heat the oil in a large (5- or 6-quart) casserole. Add the beef, a few pieces at a time to sear them. (Add more oil as needed.) When seared, remove the meat and set aside.

Add the onions and cook until transparent. Return the beef to the casserole. Add the bay leaves, garlic, salt and pepper. Add the tomatoes and enough consommé to cover. Cover tightly and bake for 2 hours.

Meanwhile, cut the pie pumpkin in half and clean out the seeds and soft matter with a large spoon. Cut the pumpkin into 1-inch-wide strips. Peel the strips off the hard outer shell and slice them into large squares.

After the beef has cooked for 2 hours, add the pumpkin, potatoes, turnips, apricots, prunes, raisins and parsley. Stir, return to the oven and continue to bake for another 15 minutes. Add the green beans and bake 15 minutes longer, stirring and testing for the doneness of the vegetables.

Prepare your "serving" pumpkin by carefully cutting the top to make a large lid. Scrape out the seeds and soft matter. Replace the lid on the pumpkin at an angle to allow the heat during baking to reach inside as well. Remove the casserole from the oven and allow it to sit, covered, while the large pumpkin heats (on a cookie sheet) for 20 minutes in the oven. Serve the stew in the pumpkin.

Variations: For a thicker dish to serve on plates, dredge the meat in flour before searing and add the consommé barely to cover.

When cauliflower is abundant, try substituting it (3 cups) for the turnips and potatoes.

(GENE BOUCHER)

Pumpkin-Apple Casserole
6–8 servings

*1½ pounds apples, peeled, cored and cut
   in ¼-inch-thick slices*
1 teaspoon lemon juice
½ cup light brown sugar
6 tablespoons butter
½ cup apple cider or juice
3 tablespoons maple syrup
1 tablespoon freshly squeezed lemon juice
1 teaspoon ground cinnamon
¼ teaspoon ground nutmeg
½ teaspoon ground ginger
3½ cups fresh pumpkin purée

Preheat the oven to 325°. Grease a shallow 2-quart baking dish.

Place the apples in water to cover with 1 teaspoon of lemon juice to prevent discoloration. Set aside.

Bring the sugar, butter, cider, maple syrup, 1 teaspoon of lemon juice, cinnamon, nutmeg and ginger to a boil in a small saucepan. Lower the heat and let simmer for 10 minutes, stirring constantly.

Drain the apples.

Put the pumpkin into the prepared baking dish. Arrange the apples in overlapping positions on top of the pumpkin. Pour the sauce over the mixture. Bake for 30 minutes, or until the apples are tender. Baste occasionally with the sauce.

Delicious with smoked ham, fresh ham or turkey.

(DIANE SCHNEIDER)

Pumpkin-Apple Ring

8 servings

2 cups all-purpose flour
1 teaspoon baking powder
½ teaspoon baking soda
¼ teaspoon salt
½ teaspoon ground cinnamon
½ teaspoon ground nutmeg
¼ teaspoon ground cloves
¼ teaspoon ground ginger
1½ cups sugar
½ cup sweet butter
2 eggs, beaten
1½ cups shredded apples
1 cup mashed cooked fresh pumpkin meat
Powdered sugar

Preheat the oven to 350°. Grease and flour an 8-inch bundt or tube pan.

Sift together the first 8 ingredients and set aside.

Cream together the sugar and butter. Add the eggs and mix well. Stir in the apples and the pumpkin. Add the dry ingredients, one third at a time, and mix very well.

Pour into the prepared pan and bake for 55 minutes, or until a knife inserted into the center comes out clean. Sift the powdered sugar over the cake before serving.

(HELEN AVENS-MARTIN)

Pumpkin Soufflé

6 servings

3 tablespoons melted butter
3 tablespoons all-purpose flour
½ teaspoon salt
½ teaspoon ground cinnamon
½ teaspoon ground nutmeg
½ teaspoon ground ginger
½ teaspoon mace
2 tablespoons grated orange rind
2 cups brown sugar
2 cups puréed cooked fresh pumpkin
3 eggs, separated
1 cup warm milk
Whipped cream

Preheat the oven to 375°. Butter a 1-quart soufflé dish.

Make a roux by heating the butter and flour in a saucepan.

Combine the salt, cinnamon, nutmeg, ginger, mace and orange rind. When thoroughly mixed, add to the roux.

Stir in the brown sugar and pumpkin. Blend in the egg yolks and milk. Simmer the mixture over low heat until it slightly thickens, about 10 minutes. Remove from the heat and let cool.

Meanwhile, beat the 3 egg whites until stiff. Fold them into the pumpkin mixture.

Pour the mixture into the prepared soufflé dish and bake for 45 minutes. Serve warm, topped with fresh whipped cream.

(**MRS. WILLIAM HAYES**)

Pumpkin Flan

6 servings

¼ cup sugar
1 cup fresh pumpkin purée, cooked
5 large eggs, beaten
½ teaspoon salt
1½ cups evaporated milk
⅓ cup water
1½ teaspoons vanilla extract
1 teaspoon ground ginger
¼ teaspoon ground nutmeg

Preheat the oven to 350°.

Caramelize the sugar by placing it in a heavy skillet over moderately high heat. Stir occasionally with a wooden spoon until the sugar begins to melt; then stir constantly until all of it has melted to a smooth caramel. It should be a rich brown color, but do not let it become too dark or it will have a bitter burnt taste. Pour the caramelized sugar into a 9½- or 10-inch pie pan. Tilt the pan to coat the bottom and sides. Continue to tilt and turn the pan until the caramel stops running. Set aside.

Combine the pumpkin and eggs in a large mixing bowl; blend well. Add the remaining ingredients, one at a time, stirring and blending thoroughly. Pour the pumpkin mixture into the caramelized pan. Place the pan in a larger pan of water and bake for 1 hour and 20 minutes, or until a knife inserted into the center comes out clean. Cool thoroughly before unmolding.

(RUTH COBBETT BIEMILLER)

Long Island Pumpkin Cake

12 servings

2 cups sugar
1¼ cups oil
1½ cups fresh pumpkin purée, cooked
4 eggs
3 cups flour
2 teaspoons baking powder
2 teaspoons baking soda
2 teaspoons ground cinnamon
1 teaspoon salt
½ cup golden raisins
½ cup dark raisins
1 cup chopped walnuts or pecans
Whipped cream

Preheat the oven to 350°. Grease and flour a 10-inch tube pan.

Combine the sugar and oil in a large mixing bowl and blend well. Stir in the pumpkin and mix thoroughly. Add the eggs, one at a time, beating well after each addition. Set aside.

Sift together the flour, baking powder, baking soda, cinnamon and salt. Fold into the cake batter. Stir in the raisins and nuts.

Pour into the prepared pan. Bake for 1¼ hours, or until done. Do not open the oven door under 1 hour! Let the cake cool in the pan before turning out onto a rack. Serve with fresh whipped cream.

(HELEN STRANG)

Pumpkin Pie
6–8 servings

2 eggs
2 cups fresh pumpkin purée, cooked
2 tablespoons flour
1 teaspoon salt
1½ teaspoons ground cinnamon
½ teaspoon ground nutmeg
½ teaspoon allspice
¼ teaspoon ground ginger
½ cup white sugar
½ cup firmly packed brown sugar
2 tablespoons brandy
1⅔ cups light cream
9-inch deep prebaked pie shell

Preheat the oven to 425°.

Beat the eggs until light. Stir in the pumpkin.

Combine the flour, salt, cinnamon, nutmeg, allspice, ginger, white sugar and brown sugar, and stir into the pumpkin mixture. Add the brandy and light cream, and mix thoroughly.

When well blended, pour the pumpkin filling into the pie shell and bake for 10 minutes. Reduce the heat to 325°, and bake for approximately 45 minutes, or until a knife inserted into the center comes out clean.

(LILA MAGIE)

Pumpkin-Pear Purée

4 servings

4 tablespoons butter
1 medium onion, finely chopped
2 cloves garlic, finely minced
2 pounds pumpkin, peeled and cut into small cubes
1 pound very ripe pears, peeled and cubed (preferably
  Crassanne, a very heavy, heady pear, what is called a
  melting pear)
1 stick cinnamon
2 whole cloves, optional
½ cup water (approximately)
Salt to taste

Melt the butter in a large, heavy skillet over low heat, add the onion and garlic, and sauté for 5 minutes, or until soft.

Add the pumpkin cubes and sauté, gently mashing them until soft, about 15 minutes. Add the pears and spices, cover and continue to simmer gently, uncovering and gently mashing the mixture about every 10 minutes. Add the water—it should just cover the mixture. Simmer, covered, until the mixture is soft, stirring occasionally. If the mixture appears too thick, uncover and allow the liquid to evaporate. Remove the spices and put the mixture through a food processor. Salt to taste.

This is a wonderful dish to be creative with; try adding cardamom, allspice and nutmeg.

(LOUISE SKLOWER)

Pumpkin Ice Cream

12 servings

2 cups mashed cooked fresh pumpkin
2 eggs
2 teaspoons ground cinnamon
½ teaspoon ground ginger
½ teaspoon allspice
2 tablespoons molasses
2 quarts softened vanilla ice cream
12 very small pumpkins

Combine the mashed pumpkin, eggs, spices and molasses in a large bowl. Stir in the ice cream and blend thoroughly. Put into a container and freeze to solidify.

Cut off the tops of the small pumpkins. Hollow out the cavity of each pumpkin and place a large muffin tin in each. When ready to serve, scoop the ice cream into the tins and replace the pumpkin tops. For a festive occasion, tie a black velvet ribbon on each stem. If possible, serve with chocolate-iced cookies in the shape of leaves. For a centerpiece, hollow out a huge pumpkin and fill with colorful autumn leaves. Great for a harvest party!

(HELEN GRAY)

SALSIFY

Salsify Sautéed with Herbs
4 servings

1 pound salsify
1 cup milk
2 tablespoons butter
1 clove garlic, crushed
1 tablespoon chopped fresh rosemary
1 tablespoon chopped fresh oregano
2 tablespoons chopped fresh parsley
Salt and freshly ground black pepper to taste
1 teaspoon freshly squeezed lemon juice

Scrape the salsify and immerse it briefly in the milk to prevent discoloration. Cut it into 1-inch cubes and cook in boiling salted water for about 15 minutes, or until just tender. Drain well and keep warm.

Melt the butter in a heavy skillet. Add the garlic and sauté for 1 minute. Add the salsify, rosemary, oregano, parsley, salt and pepper. Sauté for 6 minutes, or until the salsify is lightly browned. Transfer to a warm serving dish and sprinkle with lemon juice. Serve immediately.

TURNIPS AND RUTABAGA

Turnip Custard
6 servings

12 ounces turnips (weight after peeling)
3 ounces white potatoes (weight after peeling)
3 tablespoons unsalted butter
2 large eggs
½ cup milk
3 tablespoons evaporated skimmed milk
½ teaspoon ground nutmeg
½ teaspoon salt

Preheat the oven to 375°. Butter a 9-inch round pan.
   Boil the turnips until very tender, about 20 minutes. Drain.
   Boil the potatoes in a separate pot. Drain.
   Place the turnips and butter in a blender or food processor (use a metal blade) and process for about 10 seconds. Add all the remaining ingredients except the potatoes and process for 30 seconds.
   Put the potatoes through a fine sieve and stir into the mixture. Add more salt if necessary.
   Turn out into the prepared pan. Set it in a larger ovenproof dish with boiling water to a depth of approximately ½ inch. Place on the middle rack of the oven and bake for 40 minutes.
   Remove from the oven and let stand for 5 minutes before serving. When ready to serve, run a knife around the edge of the pan and invert onto a serving platter.
   This dish reheats remarkably well. Just put it in a barely simmering water bath on top of the stove for 30 minutes.

(LEE BAILEY)

Rutabaga Waldorf Salad

8 servings

2 cups cubed rutabaga (about 1 medium rutabaga)
2 cups cubed Mutsu or Granny Smith apples (2–3 apples)
2 cups chopped celery (3–4 stalks)
1–2 cups walnut halves (according to taste)
3 egg yolks
1 teaspoon Dijon mustard
1½–2 cups sunflower or safflower oil
2–4 tablespoons Cointreau
Boston lettuce leaves

Peel the rutabaga and cut into ½-inch cubes. Blanch in boiling salted water for about 8 minutes. Drain and cool.

Peel and core the apples. Cut into ½-inch cubes. Combine the rutabaga, apple, celery and walnuts in a large bowl. Set aside.

Using a wire whisk, combine the egg yolks and mustard. Gradually add the oil, making a very thick mayonnaise. Blend in the Cointreau, a tablespoon at a time, until the dressing is thinned to the consistency of mayonnaise.

Dress the salad and serve on a bed of Boston lettuce leaves.

(DANA JACOBI)

Julienne Turnips, Rutabaga and Carrots

6 servings

½ pound turnips
½ pound rutabaga
½ pound carrots
4 tablespoons sweet butter
¼ teaspoon nutmeg
2 tablespoons freshly squeezed lemon juice
Salt and freshly ground black pepper to taste
1 teaspoon minced fresh chives for garnish

Peel and cut the turnips, rutabaga and carrots into 2 × ¼-inch strips. Steam the vegetables for 10 minutes.

Melt the butter in a heavy skillet and blend in the nutmeg and lemon juice. Transfer the vegetables to the skillet and toss with the butter mixture until well blended. Remove from the heat and season with salt and pepper. Garnish with fresh minced chives and serve.

(BETTY PELL)

WINTER SQUASH

Spaghetti Squash Primavera
6 servings

2 large ripe tomatoes, finely chopped
1 cup diced cucumbers
½ cup fresh chopped parsley
½ cup finely chopped fresh basil
½ cup diced red onions
½ cup salad oil
Juice of 1 lemon
1 clove garlic, crushed
1 3-pound spaghetti squash
4 quarts boiling water
Dash of salt and freshly ground black pepper
Freshly grated Parmesan cheese

Place the tomatoes, cucumbers, parsley, basil and onions in a large bowl. Combine the oil, lemon juice and garlic and pour over the vegetables. Mix well and set aside to marinate.

Place the spaghetti squash in the boiling water and cook for 15 minutes. Prick it in four places with a fork and continue cooking for another 30 minutes. Remove the squash. Let cool for 5 minutes, then cut in half lengthwise and scoop out the seeds. Using a fork, pull out the strands of "spaghetti."

Mix the spaghetti with the well-marinated vegetables. Season with salt and pepper. Sprinkle with freshly grated Parmesan cheese before serving.

(JEAN DETRE)

Turk's Turban à l'Indienne

4–6 servings

1 1-pound Turk's turban squash
2 tablespoons butter or sesame oil
1 medium onion, coarsely chopped
⅓ cup pine nuts or coarsely chopped
   walnuts or almonds
¼ cup currants or raisins
¼ teaspoon ground cumin
¼ teaspoon turmeric
2 tablespoons chopped fresh coriander
2 cups cooked brown rice

Preheat the oven to 350°.

Cut the topknot off the squash for a lid. Scoop out the seeds and stringy pulp, leaving a cavity into which the rice mixture will be stuffed. Discard the seeds and pulp. Set the squash aside.

Melt the butter in a large heavy skillet over low heat, add the onions and sauté until soft and transparent. Add the remaining ingredients and stir until well blended.

Fill the squash cavity with the mixture, cover with the topknot and bake for ¾–1 hour. Serve by cutting the squash like a cake in wedges.

(SUSAN WOOD)

Winter Squash Soup

8 servings

4 tablespoons olive oil
4 tablespoons butter
6 shallots, minced
1 tablespoon chopped fresh rosemary
*3½ pounds butternut squash, peeled and chopped
  (about 8 cups)*
¾ pound parsnips, peeled and chopped (about 2½ cups)
7 cups chicken broth
1 cup heavy cream
Salt and freshly ground black pepper to taste

Heat the oil and butter in a large heavy pot until the butter melts. Add the shallots and rosemary, and sauté for 2 minutes over medium heat. Add the squash and parsnips. Cover and continue to cook for 20 minutes, stirring frequently.

Add the chicken broth. Bring to a boil, reduce the heat to medium and continue to cook, covered, until the vegetables are tender, about 10 minutes.

Purée in a food processor or blender and return to the pot. Add the cream and season with salt and pepper. Blend well. Ladle into warm soup bowls and serve with a crusty sourdough bread.

Baked Acorn Squash

6 servings

3 medium acorn squash
6 tablespoons melted butter
⅓ cup pure maple syrup
3 tablespoons light brown sugar
1 teaspoon ground cinnamon
¼ teaspoon ground nutmeg

Preheat the oven to 400°.

Halve the squash, and remove the seeds and stringy portion. Cut off and discard a small slice from the bottom of each squash so it will sit flat. Place the halves cut side down in a baking dish with ½ inch water and bake for 30 minutes.

Combine the butter, maple syrup, brown sugar and spices. Turn the squash cut side up and divide the butter mixture evenly among the squash cavities. Continue to bake for 25–30 minutes, or until tender. Remove from the oven and serve.

Golden Stuffing

6–8 servings

1 piece fresh ginger, 2–3 inches long
1 cup sugar
2 cups water
1 medium acorn squash
8 tablespoons sweet butter
2 large (or 3 medium) leeks
4–6 shallots
2 navel oranges
1 pound seasoned bread stuffing
½–1 cup chicken stock
Salt and freshly ground black pepper to taste

Preheat the oven to 400°.

Peel and finely dice the fresh ginger. Remove the bitterness by blanching as follows. Bring 2–3 cups of water to a boil and add the diced ginger. Let boil for 5 minutes. Drain and repeat.

Combine the sugar and water, and bring to a boil to create a light syrup. Add the blanched ginger, bring to a boil, and boil gently for 20–30 minutes, letting the syrup evaporate and the ginger "candy." Drain and, if necessary, rinse under cold running water so the pieces are not stuck together. Set aside.

Cut the acorn squash lengthwise, remove the seeds and peel. Chop into ¼-inch pieces, making about 3 cups of chopped raw squash. In the oven, melt 3–4 tablespoons of the butter on a baking sheet with raised edges. Add the chopped squash and stir until all the pieces are lightly coated with the melted butter. Bake the squash until the pieces are barely tender, about 10 minutes, stirring often to prevent browning. Set aside.

Cut off the green part of the leeks and discard. Cut the remaining white section lengthwise and wash under running water to remove all the sand, then dice into ¼-inch pieces. Peel the shallots and dice into ¼-inch pieces. Using the remaining butter, bake the leeks and shallots in the same manner as the squash for about 10 minutes, stirring occasionally, and set aside.

Reduce the oven to 350°.

Peel and cut the navel oranges into ¼-inch pieces.

In a large bowl, combine the cooked squash, leeks, shallots, and ginger. Add the stuffing in an amount roughly equal to the volume of the ingredients already in the bowl (less stuffing makes a lighter dish, more makes a heavier, denser dish). Add the diced orange with its juice, then moisten the mixture with the warm stock until it is lightly moistened and fluffy. Season with salt and pepper.

Transfer to a buttered ovenproof baking dish. Bake, uncovered, for approximately 30–40 minutes, until the top is brown and crusty.

This dish is lighter than traditional stuffing recipes. Its flavor is a mellow complexity of spicy ginger, rich leeks and shallots, and the acid tang of oranges against the traditional herbs of a bread stuffing.

(DANA JACOBI)

Winter Squash Bread

8 servings

1 cup white sugar
½ cup brown sugar
1 cup mashed cooked winter squash
½ cup oil
2 eggs, beaten
¼ cup water
2 cups all-purpose flour
1 teaspoon baking soda
½ teaspoon salt
½ teaspoon ground nutmeg
½ teaspoon ground cinnamon
¼ teaspoon ground ginger
1 cup raisins
½ cup chopped pecans

Preheat the oven to 350°.

In a mixing bowl, combine the white sugar, brown sugar, squash, oil, eggs and water, and blend well.

Sift together the flour, baking soda, salt, nutmeg, cinnamon and ginger. Gradually stir the dry ingredients, one third at a time, into the squash mixture. Mix well. Stir in the raisins and nuts.

Spoon into a greased and floured 9 × 5 × 3-inch loaf pan. Bake for 55–65 minutes, or until a knife inserted into the center comes out clean. Cool in the pan for 10 minutes, then turn out on a rack and cool.

(HELEN AVENS-MARTIN)

INDEX